warriorchicks

rising strong,
beautiful &
confident

D0104580

holly wagner

Regal

From Gospel Light
Ventura, California, U.S.A.

Published by Regal Books

From Gospel Light

Ventura, California, U.S.A.

Library of Congress Cataloging-in-Publication Data

Wagner, Holly.

  Warrior chicks : rising strong, beautiful, and confident / Holly Wagner.

     p. cm.

  ISBN 978-0-8307-4480-0 (trade paper)

  1. Christian women—Religious life. I. Title.

  BV4527.W298 2007

  248.8'43—dc22

                                                              2007006373

1 2 3 4 5 6 7 8 9 10 / 10 09 08 07

Rights for publishing this book in other languages are contracted by Gospel Light Worldwide, the international nonprofit ministry of Gospel Light. For additional information, visit www.gospellightworldwide.org.

dedicated to Leslie,
one of the bravest warrior chicks I know

I loved *Warrior Chicks*! Holly did a great job in communicating the picture of women being strong and standing up to fight.

LTC Beth Garrity Marchman
U.S. Army (Retired)

contents

Thanks 6

Introduction 7

Chapter 1 11
Bellisima!

Chapter 2 21
Rise and Shine!

Chapter 3 37
Stay at Your Post!

Chapter 4 54
Focus!

Chapter 5 67
The Baton Exchange

Chapter 6 77
Never Alone

Chapter 7 97
Get Dressed!

Chapter 8 117
Who's the Boss?

Chapter 9 136
Ready or Not . . .

Chapter 10 156
More Than

Chapter 11 174
Braveheart

Some Last Thoughts 194

Warrior Chicks Study Guide . . 198

Endnotes 205

thanks

I am thankful for so many things . . .

Thank you to my God, for showing me the path of life.

Thank you to my husband, for the encouragement and the never-ending love.

Thank you to Jordan and Paris, for letting me tell your stories.

Thank you to my Oasis family, for your support as I continue to work out the way of the warrior.

To Ashley, for the thoughts.

To Lisa, for the help.

To my friends, for the endorsements.

To my fellow warriors, for your stories.

introduction

I have always been told, "You have to choose your battles." This is probably good advice in marriage and parenting—however, some battles I've had to fight, I did not choose.

They chose me.

I did not choose to battle cancer.

But I knew that in order to survive it, I had to fight.

There is a verse in Proverbs 31 that used to annoy me.

It said that I had to rise "while it is yet night." *What?*

I do my best sleeping while it is "yet night," don't you?

But I found out that verse has more to say than just the time of day you get up. It has everything to do with being a woman who "rises" in the midst of hard times. When darkness and chaos abound, the woman, the warrior—*you*—rise.

I think our world is looking and waiting for a company of people who will rise in the midst of hard times. It would be so much easier to sit, to give in, to give up.

I know.

We have all felt like that.

We can't make the mistake of thinking that we are living in peacetime. We are not civilians.

We are either a casualty or a warrior.

Choose.

But how about if together, we decide to be those women who rise? I will if you will.

As a nation, we may not have wanted to enter the fight against terrorism, and whether or not you agree with the methods our country is using, we can probably all agree that it is a battle worth fighting.

You and I may or may not face actual invaders into our homeland, but we will all face battles. Whether we ever wear camouflage or not, being warriors is in our DNA. And the better we are at being warriors, the more equipped we will be at winning the battles we have been destined to win from all eternity.

Did you enlist in this battle . . . or were you drafted?

"Soldier" is a position.

"Warrior" is an attitude . . .

Benjamin Martin, in the movie *The Patriot,* wanted nothing more to do with battles.

He had seen enough bloodshed in his life.

He just wanted a simple life.

He wanted to live in peace with his family. (Don't we all?)

He changed his mind and entered the American Revolution when his son was killed and his home burned down.

The cause, which had been big and impersonal, now became personal. So he entered the war. He realized that some things are worth fighting for.

He enlisted.

My friend knew that there were thousands of unwanted babies dying of AIDS. It broke her heart.

She kept waiting for someone to do something.

She waited.

The need was so great.

Who would help?

She waited.

She heard a voice from heaven: "You help."

So she did.

She started orphanages to take them in.

She enlisted.

I know the tragedy cancer brings.

It knows no age restrictions.

It makes no distinctions based on ethnicity.

I knew it had killed millions and fighting it was certainly a worthy cause to financially support. I had just never entered the battle, not until it touched my life.

Only then did I walk to raise money.

Only then did I begin educating myself on health and nutrition.

Only then did I directly start influencing the people in my world to make lifestyle and health changes.

Only then did I consume massive quantities of wheatgrass and kombucha. (Don't ask.)

The war had touched me personally, so I became a warrior.

I was drafted.

Are you facing a disintegrating marriage?

Are you worried about the decisions your teenager is making?

Are you losing the battle of faith?

Does the plight of the orphaned children in Africa touch you?

Are you wondering if you will ever get married?

Are you angered over the plight of young girls who are kidnapped into the sex trade?

Are you uncertain about your career direction?

Does the unwed, pregnant teenager move you with compassion?

Is your health in crisis?

Has your heart been broken?

Hello, soldier.

Welcome to life as a warrior.

chapter 1

bellisima!

You are so beautiful, my beloved, so perfect in every part.
Song of Solomon 4:7, *NLT*

Screams are heard all over the community.

A young woman is awakened from sleep.

Wave after wave of fear spreads through homes as a vicious band of terrorizing outlaws invades her homeland.

Her aging father receives orders to rejoin the army and go fight the invaders.

Her heart breaks as she sees him accept the orders.

He limps into the house in order to prepare to join the battle in the morning.

Later that night she quietly sneaks into her father's closet and takes his armor.

He is too old for this battle, so she will fight on his behalf.

She uses his sword to cut her beautiful long black hair. She wraps a cloth around her chest, concealing her breasts. She puts on her father's armor, picks up his sword, mounts her horse and stealthily leaves her home in the middle of the night.

Knowing that her deception could cost her life, still she directs her horse to the camp of soldiers who are training for war.

When she arrives, the soldiers do not see a woman. They see a young boy. She maintains the disguise as she prepares for battle.

She becomes a fierce warrior and is part of some great victories. Yet only when her disguise comes off and her fellow soldiers see her as the woman she is does she achieve her greatest triumph: saving the emperor.

Thank you, Mulan.

The Nazgul, a servant of the enemy, races to destroy the king of Rohan.

The flying beast's ugly face is fierce and determined.

Princess Eowyn knows that in order for this battle to be won, everyone must do his or her part.

She puts on her armor and heads to the battlefield. She knows the Nazgul is going after her uncle, the king, so she races into the battle.

The Nazgul taunts her, saying, "You don't get between me and my enemy."

As the princess waves her sword, he continues the taunt. "No man can kill me!"

She boldly proclaims, "I am no man!" (I love that part.)

Then she stabs him. (That part's not bad either!)

He falls to the ground, never to rise again.

You rule, Eowyn!

Her people have been oppressed for years.

They are tired and afraid.

Now a new enemy threatens them.

While the armies battle it out, the enemy leader escapes.

He comes to her tent.

She is probably terrified.

Despite what she fears, she offers him refreshment and a place to rest.

While he is sleeping, she looks around for a weapon.

She can't find her husband's armor.

And his sword is nowhere to be seen.

She looks for something she can use.

She spies a tent peg and a hammer.

A tent peg.

Could it be that easy?

She approaches the enemy and hammers the tent peg through his temple.

Using what she had, she defeated the enemy.

Way to go, Jael.

I am not sure why we always think that someone else's armor would be better.

Someone else always looks more qualified.

If I could just look like her, *then* I would be beautiful.

If I just had what he had, *then* I would be successful.

We question whether we can really win this battle simply with what we have—ourselves.

Why is it that we feel the need to be someone else? Why don't we see ourselves as good enough?

Well, I don't have all the answers.

But I do have a few thoughts . . . (shocking, I know!).

If I were the enemy, devising a strategy to defeat humankind, the first thing I would do is make people question their ability. I would lie to them so that they would doubt their purpose. I would keep them focused on their weaknesses so that they would never harness their strength.

I remember hearing about POWs in Vietnam who were tortured to extract classified information. One of the tools that the enemy used was deception. The torturer would say, "Your country has forgotten all about you. You don't matter to them." If the enemy could get the captured soldier to believe that, then they could probably get the information they needed. And it all started with a lie.

We do have an enemy. His greatest weapons are lies and deceptions. In fact, his only weapons are lies and deceptions.

He looks for our weaknesses and then attacks. Don't become his prisoner. He can make you think . . .

That man would be better for me than my husband.

I deserve this sickness.

There are so many problems in the world. Nothing I do will make a difference.I

I can cheat on my taxes; everyone does.

I don't deserve to be loved.

I am not enough.

I don't have what it takes.

All lies.

If the enemy can get us to believe his lies, he can win a battle or two.

If he can get you to question God's love for you . . .

If he can cause you to look in the mirror and see failure . . .

If he can get you to doubt who you are . . .

. . . he might be able to stop you from fulfilling your purpose.

Don't believe the lies.

A recent issue of *People* magazine featured a list of the "World's Most Beautiful People." When interviewed on television, one of the editors said that beauty was "obvious."

Obvious to whom?

Who determines what makes someone beautiful?

The editors of a magazine?

I don't think so.

Most of us look at fashion magazines and feel depressed shortly afterward. Why? Because we feel as if we can never measure up. When we look in the mirror, our imperfections shout loudly at us.

"Big pimple in middle of forehead!"

"Serious baggage under eyes!"

"Very large nose!"

"Lots of crow's feet!"

"Disappearing lips!"

Those women in the magazines look perfect. But I would like to let you in on a little secret—shhhh—the women in those photos aren't perfect, either. I know.

Because I was once one of them.

I showed up on modeling assignments looking anything but perfect. It took hours of hair and makeup geniuses, hemorrhoid cream on puffy eyes, tape to hold everything together, Photoshop to get rid of the pimples—all to create an illusion. Honestly, there were times when the image was so fictitious it might as well have been a cartoon![1]

If we are to become effective warriors, the first war we must win is the war to believe that we are beautiful. And these battles are fought on the inside. We can certainly change our outer appearance and use weapons to wage a war against aging, but unless we conquer the battle to see ourselves as beautiful, external changes won't help.

I recently interviewed Jennifer Strickland, who at one time was a model for the designer Armani. She told stories of the price she, and other young women, paid to look "perfect." Every single young model she encountered was either using drugs or dealing with a serious eating disorder.

She told of one model who was known for her smile.

In fact, her smile graced many billboards advertising toothpaste.

She looked "perfect" and happy.

In reality, she threw up nine or ten times a day and was desperately unhappy.

She looked in the mirror and saw flaws.

She saw what she wasn't.

I have read articles and heard various news stories of women around the world who are desperately trying to change themselves into some elusive image of beauty. There are young girls in Japan who are putting steel rods in their legs because they think that taller is beautiful.

Who said?

There are women in India who are paying to have their skin lightened because they think lighter is beautiful.

Who said?

There are some Asian women having surgery to have their eyes made rounder.

Who said that round eyes were more beautiful?

Why is it that we always see someone else as more beautiful?

The only way to defeat this way of thinking is to look in the mirror and shout (go ahead, shout it out loud!):

> *I praise you [God] because of the wonderful way you created me. Everything you do is marvelous! Of this I have no doubt!*[2]

In fact, why don't you just whistle at yourself right after you shout! We were created in the image of our Creator, and He calls us beautiful . . . marvelous. Every curve, freckle and strand of hair is beautiful.

I get this picture of God right after He created us. He looks at us and does the Italian thing with his fingers against his lips, shouting, "*Bellisima . . . perfecto!*"

God has declared that we are marvelous . . . beautiful.

Yet we don't really believe it, so we look and wait for someone else to tell us. Some of us dress in such a way to show every curve and all our cleavage (if we are lucky enough to have some ☺), hoping that someone will say we are beautiful. But our Creator has already said it! You *are* beautiful. No matter the shape of your eyes, the size of your nose, the color of your skin, the texture of your hair or the smoothness of your skin—you are beautiful!

Most of us have probably seen the movie *Shrek*. At the end of the movie, after a "true love's" kiss, Fiona is disappointed to find out that she has not turned back into a woman, but instead remained an ogre. She looks at Shrek and says, "I was supposed to be beautiful." He replies, "But you *are* beautiful."

You and I have been given "true love's" kiss by our Creator. And He says we are beautiful.

Jesus told us that one of the most important things we can do is love other people. In fact He said that we are to love them as we love ourselves.

We probably do.

That may be why we are not that great at loving others—because we are not that great at loving ourselves.

I wonder if it isn't a slap in God's face when we don't like who He made us to be and want something else. Yes, we are supposed to learn from those around us, but we are not to try to become them! We each have a role to play on the planet, and we will only be effective at doing it if we are comfortable in our own skin.

Being inspired by other people is good.

Comparing ourselves to others is not.

We can never be anyone else.

We can only be who God made us to be!

A water-bearer carries two large pots on a yoke across his shoulders up the hill from the river to his master's house each day. One has a crack and leaks half its water out each day before arriving at the house. The other pot is perfect and always delivers a full portion of water after the long walk from the river.

Finally, after years of arriving half-empty and feeling guilty, the cracked pot apologized to the water-bearer. It was miserable. "I'm sorry that I couldn't accomplish what the perfect pot did."

The water-bearer said, "What do you have to apologize for?"

"After all this time, I still only deliver half my load of water. I make more work for you because of my flaw."

The man smiled and told the pot. "Take note of all the lovely flowers growing on the side of the path where I carried you. The flowers grew so lovely because of the water you leaked. There are no flowers on the perfect pot's side."[3]

I would first like to say that there is no "perfect" pot. All of us have a past or hurts or issues we are dealing with.

The point is that our past—or what we might see as flaws—can create beauty. You and I must understand, really understand, all the way to our core, that we are beautiful. Just the way we are.

Only when we realize this will we be able to extend our hand to help—which is one of the reasons we are still breathing. We were created to join God in doing the work He does, the good work we had better be doing.[4] Believe it or not, God is counting on you and me to co-labor with Him to bring His love and goodness to the planet. We are not just spectators; we are participants. And being a participant in His army makes us soldiers. And if we choose, we can become a warrior—and since we are beautiful, that makes us beautiful warriors!

I think there is a difference between a soldier and a warrior. Being a soldier is perhaps a good place to start. Every army is made up of soldiers. As soldiers, we are positioning ourselves for battle. That's good. It is certainly better than the position of spectator.

A soldier is a person who serves in an army, a person engaged in military service. This word comes from the Old French word *soudoior* and is derived from the French coin named *sou*. A *soudoior* was a man who fought for pay.

There is nothing wrong with being paid to fight. Our soldiers currently engaged in battle around the world are drawing a salary. But if we are going to win the war, soldiers must become warriors.

A warrior is one who is engaged aggressively in or experienced in battle. A warrior possesses the dedication that money can't buy. A warrior is someone who fights, not because of what she is getting out of it, but because of what she can give. A warrior is a soldier with a "die for the cause" attitude. A warrior will do whatever it takes to ensure victory. A soldier signs up to join the fight; a warrior stays until it is finished.

I heard a Marine recently say that during wartime the number of people volunteering or signing up to join the armed services drops significantly. Most are just interested in the GI Bill. They don't mind joining the army; they just don't want to go to war. It seems that not as many want to participate while the battles are raging. Sometimes I wonder if this isn't like lots of Christians (not us, of course!) who want the benefits of serving God but don't really want to pay the price. People who want the results of victory without ever lifting their sword. Not sure that will happen.

We won the American Revolution, not because our soldiers were better trained, but because our soldiers became warriors. The British were not fighting for their homeland—we were. As a rag-tag group of warriors, we defeated highly trained soldiers. We did whatever it took to gain freedom.

Soldiers became warriors as they walked miles with no shoes.

Soldiers became warriors as they suffered a winter in Valley Forge with no blankets and very little food.

Soldiers became warriors as they trained day after day in the snow.

I am asking you to begin the journey toward becoming a warrior. It is the only way we can win the battles that life throws our way. And you're not becoming just any warrior—but a beautiful one.

It is in your DNA.

> *If you know the enemy and know yourself, you need not fear the result of a hundred battles. If you know yourself, but not the enemy, for every victory gained you will also suffer a defeat. If you know neither the enemy nor yourself, you will succumb in every battle.*
>
> Sun Tzu[5]

chapter 2

rise and shine!

They were the pampered wives of British, Australian and American military officers and businessmen living in Singapore in 1942. When the Japanese forces took control of the city, many of them ended up in a prison camp.

They were brutalized.

They were tortured.

They almost starved.

One was executed for trying to get medicine to her dying friend. Another was tortured for speaking the truth.

In desperation, one woman gathered the others and started a vocal orchestra as an attempt to bring joy to their hearts.

Each woman, alto or soprano, had a part.

They spent hours practicing notes.

The music gave them purpose.

In the midst of devastation and horror, music could be heard and spirits were lifted.

Hope was restored and many of the women survived to be rescued three years later.

Thank you to the warriors of Paradise Road.

Warriors, somehow, manage to find joy in the midst of darkness.

There will be trials and dark moments that you and I face in life.

They come to the good and the bad, to the just and the unjust.

Trials come to us all.

They are not optional.

They are part of the curriculum of life. (Shoot!)

Trials and challenges are very evident in our world, our country, our city, our families and within our own heart. Jesus promised us that in this world we would have trials, distress and frustration, but that we should be at peace because He has overcome the world for us—showing us how to get victory![1]

Being at peace in the midst of a dark moment is much easier said than done. I am aware of that!

One of my favorite Bible verses says, "in Christ, God leads us from place to place in one perpetual victory parade."[2] I am certainly not a Bible scholar, but I have learned a few things about that verse. Paul was referring to the victory parade Caesar gave when one of his Roman generals succeeded in a military campaign. In this parade there was dancing, music, cheering . . . and maybe confetti! The conquering general rode in a great chariot pulled by white horses, and his army followed. They all shared in the glory of the celebration Caesar threw on behalf of the victorious military leader. What an awesome sight it must have been!

The picture for you and me is this: Jesus is our conquering General. You and I are part of His army—the warrior chicks!—and share in the victory. He leads us in one perpetual victory parade.

We need to see ourselves riding in the parade. We are not trudging through a world of misery. We'd better practice our parade wave and get the smile ready.

Of course, life is not just one great mountaintop experience after another.

Yes, we will face battles.

And yet, we are still in the victory parade.

Jesus paid a great price for us to walk in the parade, so let's do it!

God's intention, no matter what battle we face, is for us to overcome.

Isaiah challenges me every time I read what he wrote: He said that we are to *arise* from the depression in which circumstances have kept us—rise to a new life.[3]

In fact, we are supposed to shine!

He said that darkness is covering the earth (boy, isn't that the truth?), but that the glory of our God will be visible in you and me so that people who are hurting can come to us for answers.

Most of us lead full, busy lives. There are dreams and goals in our hearts. The journey to reach our dreams can be difficult, to say the least! Sometimes it is absolutely painful and scary. When you encounter a trial, don't take it personally.

I visited my daughter's science fair and learned something interesting. (One thing I learned was that either there was a lot of parental help, or those sixth-graders were geniuses!) In 1991, eight scientists created an artificial environment located in Oracle, Arizona, called Biosphere 2 and lived inside it for two years (how they managed without a shoe store and a Starbucks is beyond me!). Inside their self-sustaining community, the scientists created a number of mini-ecosystems, including a desert, rain forest and even an ocean. They simulated nearly every weather condition except wind. After a while, the effects of their windless environment became apparent. A number of trees bent over and even snapped. Without the stress of wind to strengthen the wood, the trunks grew weak and could not hold up their own weight. Like it or not, weathering trials is what builds our strength.

(Again, shoot—I wish times of celebration were what make us stronger. Don't you?)

Perhaps all this weathering storms has made you feel a bit worn, a bit tarnished.

Maybe you feel you've lost value.

But you're wrong.

Once when my husband visited an antique coin dealer, the owner told him that most people make the mistake of cleaning all of their old coins before bringing them in to sell. They think that if the coins are clean, they will be more valuable. They are wrong. Rather than calling the black stuff on old coins "tarnish," we should call it "being toned." Toning actually makes them worth *more*.

So, if you're feeling tarnished, I would like to suggest that we are merely toned—and thus growing in value. The battle you are in is toning you. It can be your ceiling in life or a stepping-stone to your future.

Your choice.

In life, we will all face setbacks. We will probably all get a small taste of failure. But we must not raise a white flag. We must not surrender. We must not concede. The whole fight is *not* over!

From 1914 to 1916, Ernest Shackleton and his men survived the wreck of their ship, *Endurance,* in the crushing Antarctic ice.

They were stranded 1,200 miles from civilization with no means of communication and no hope for rescue.

The temperatures were so low the men could hear the water freeze.

They subsisted on a diet of penguins, dogs and seals.

And when the ice began to break up, Shackleton set out to save them all on his heroic 800-mile trip across the frigid South Atlantic.

In little more than a row boat.

Unlike most other polar expeditions, every man survived . . . not only in good health, but also in good spirits . . . all due to the leadership of Shackleton.[4]

I hate being cold.

I also don't like the thought of being in bad weather—much less being *frozen* in it for two years (which are two of the reasons I live in Southern California!).

Ernest Shackleton and his crew were stuck in the Antarctic for just that long.

They not only survived.

They also came out strong.

Why?

One of the reasons is that Ernest remembered to laugh.

He encouraged his crew to play as well as work together.

They performed skits, held sing-alongs and celebrated birthdays.

Ernest was not blind to the challenge before them—he just knew that if they were going to survive, he had not only to rise, to have joy, but also to give it away.

It was more than a feeling.

It was a decision.

Remember the proverb that challenges us "to rise while it is yet night"? Do you think He might be talking to us?

When our world, our country, our city or our family is in the midst of chaos, we are supposed to rise—not wilt. We are to become strong in the midst of trials.

One of my favorite songs goes like this . . .

Lord I'm tired of doin' things my own way
With my own life, runnin' day to day

You said Your grace is enough
And Your mercy is always new
I hear your voice, it's callin'
It's callin' me to you

So I rise
Lifting my eyes I look to you
I'm alive
Living my life to honor You

Take my life
Take all I am
I'm reachin' out so take my hand

You said Your grace is enough
And Your mercy is always new
I hear Your voice, it's callin'
It's callin' me to you

So I rise
Lifting my eyes I look to you
I'm alive
Living my life to honor You

I don't know what changes life may bring
But with Your strength, I'll take on anything
Not my will, but Yours be done

So I rise . . .[5]

(If you'd like to hear the song, you can download it for free from Godchicks.com. Just put in the secret code GC2020.)

There are a number of times in the Bible when a woman rose up to bring strength in the midst of darkness . . .

There had been a total breakdown of order in Israel.

The Israelites cried out to God.

He heard their cry. (He *always* hears our cry.)

In those days of oppression, it seemed no one would come to their rescue.

At least not until Deborah rose.

Until she arose like a mother in Israel.[6]

God used her to lead the Israelites to freedom. She was just a girl, like you and me, given an opportunity to rise in the midst of a trial. She accepted the challenge and encouraged military leaders to victory.

And another woman rises . . .

She had been orphaned.

Her future looked bleak.

Until she caught the attention of a king.

She became his queen.

I wonder if there weren't moments when she thought she had it made—a real fairy-tale ending to a life that had a rough beginning.

Then she heard about a plot to destroy her people.

Maybe she had been made queen for "such a time as this."[7]

Unsummoned, Esther risked her life to approach her husband, the king.

She told him about the danger to her people and asked for his help.

And help he did.

Because of her courage, a nation of people was saved.

A real fairy-tale ending after all.

These legendary lives are just two of the women who are now part of the company cheering us on. They did their part in this grand adventure of faith.

Now it is our turn.[8]

Really, in the midst of a tough time, we have two choices.

We can be a whiner.

Or a warrior.

I am not sure there is much middle ground.

Whiners are the ones who collapse under pressure and then get mad at God for the trial. These are the ones who, when they get knocked down by life, stay there. And perhaps when you try to help, they give you all sorts of reasons why your suggestions won't work for them.

We have to be careful that their story doesn't suck us in.

We all face battles, only they wear theirs on their face—bitter and angry at the trials they have gone through.

How about we all just agree . . . *no whining*! (It doesn't help anyway!)

I began taking karate, mainly because I was watching my son take it.

Plus it just looked like fun.

And I had seen the movie *Karate Kid* . . . and was so impressed with that amazing move he did at the end of the movie. You know, the one where he was standing on one leg with his arms out—and then he let loose with a kick that felled his opponent. Well, that looked like fun. I wanted to do that!

So I showed up to class in my stiff white uniform, waiting to learn an exciting move.

We didn't learn one.

Do you know what we learned for *weeks*?

We learned how to fall.

We learned how to fall to the front and get back up, to the back and get back up, to the side and get back up. We did this at every class.

Maybe now we could do the exciting move.

Nope.

Next, we learned how to block a punch. A punch to the face. A punch to the gut.

Maybe it was finally time for the big move they had pictured on their brochure?

Nope.

Next, we learned how to block a kick.

A kick to the face.

A kick to the gut.

All of this was just a bit annoying and not glamorous at all! This was not what I had signed up for. This was not what I had seen in the brochure!

I felt like Judy Benjamin, the character that Goldie Hawn played in the movie *Private Benjamin*. After she took a look at the barracks she had been assigned to and experienced the work of a real soldier, she said, "I think they sent me to the wrong place. See, I did join the army, but I joined a *different* army. I joined the one with the condos and the private rooms."

Eventually we did do the exciting stuff. And four years later, as I was sparring and training for my black belt, I realized why we had devoted so much time to falling and getting back up. In a fight, whenever I was swept to the floor (sadly it happened more than once!), I got right back up. It was instinctive. Getting up after falling was second nature.

A proverb says that if we faint in the day of adversity, our strength is small.[9] So if we let emotion rule us, if we do not rise, then our life will be defined by the falling. I would rather my life be defined by the getting up.

It is our obligation, as daughters of the King, to rise in the midst of trials and not let them destroy us.

The world is watching.

Let's show them the strength of God in us.

We may not face the challenges that Deborah and Esther did, but each of us will face our own dark moments—our own trials that must be overcome. The decisions and choices we make at these moments are crucial if we are going to persevere.

Warriors don't freak out (at least not for long!) when they encounter a trial. Can you imagine the warriors currently representing our country freaking out every time they hear a missile explode or a gun go off? No, they just carry on with their task.

Warriors do not complain or whine or try to get you to feel sorry for them. Somehow warriors manage to find joy in the midst of their scariest times. The apostle James challenges us this way:

> Consider it a sheer gift, friends, when tests and challenges come at you from all sides. You know that under pressure, your faith-life is forced into the open and shows its true colors. So don't try to get out of anything prematurely. Let it do its work so you become mature and well-developed, not deficient in any way.[10]

A sheer gift! Is he kidding?

This doesn't mean that we pretend the challenge is not happening.

I think it means that somehow we look for something we can find joy in, just as Ria did.

Ria is an amazing woman.

After you read her story, you will think so too.

One afternoon, Ria and her husband went shopping. Their 17-year-old son, Marco, who had recently returned from boarding school, their 13-year-old daughter and their maid remained at home.

One of Marco's childhood friends forced his way into the home. This old friend had become a drug addict and was jealous of the love and affection of Marco's family. He came into the home, took a knife and killed Marco. Before leaving, he raped the maid and locked her in the closet.

The daughter remained unaware of what was going on. She was in her room with headphones on and miraculously escaped the violent rampage. When it was getting close to dinnertime, she came out of her room and noticed all the blood. She phoned her parents, screaming, "Come home now! Something has happened to Marco!" They came home to find their son dead.

Can you imagine anything worse?

The murderer was prosecuted and is in jail today.

When I met Ria she was a cheerful, energetic, generous, funny lady. There was no evidence that two years ago her world had been shattered. I asked her how she did it.

She told me that her life was like a coin. There are two sides to every coin and we can choose which side to look at. She could live the rest of her life looking at the side of the coin depicting her son's death or the side of the coin portraying the protection of her daughter. She chose to be grateful that her daughter had been spared.

Wow.

Could you do that?

A real warrior.

How amazing that you and I share this planet with someone as amazing as warrior Ria.

In January 2005, after a lumpectomy, I was diagnosed with breast cancer.

I was sure the doctor was wrong.

I couldn't have cancer.

Cancer attacked other people, not me.

This was not part of the path I had envisioned for my life.

Finally I had to practice what I preach.

(Shoot!)

It was definitely easier to preach it!

Let me be clear.

I did not want this battle.

I did not sign up for this.

I cried off and on for a few days, and then at one point I realized that I had to rise (guess my karate training kicked in!). I realized that I am a warrior and that in order to win this battle, I must rise. Wilting and whining really were not options for me. I could not yield. So I got up and began the battle.

The rising that we must do starts on the inside.

King David and his army returned home from battle to find out that the enemy had not only invaded their home, but they had also taken their wives and children.

> David and his men burst out in loud wails—wept and wept until they were exhausted with weeping. David's two wives, Ahinoam of Jezreel and Abigail widow of Nabal of Carmel, had been taken prisoner along with the rest. And suddenly David was in even worse trouble. There was talk among the men, bitter over the loss of their families, of stoning him.[11]

It makes me feel good that the first response of David and his men on encountering such a loss was that they cried until they could cry no more. Tears were one of my initial responses to the diagnosis of cancer. I cried until I was exhausted.

Have you been there?

Have you suffered such a loss or heartbreak that you wept until you had no more tears?

Not only was David heartbroken at his loss, but now his friends were blaming him. They wanted to kill him. This was not a pretty situation. But David did something that should be an encouragement to us.

He got up!

He had been knocked down and overwhelmed on the outside. But on the inside he made the decision to rise. He strengthened himself by looking to God rather than his loss.[12]

Then he rallied his army. Together they went to recover their families and all they had lost.

I think we can't just sit around and wait for God to change our circumstances. We have to first rise on the inside. Trusting that our God wants to deliver us.

Roman soldiers beat Paul and Silas to within an inch of their lives. Bleeding and in serious pain, they found themselves in prison. Somehow in this horror, they began to look to God. They started singing to Him.

Wow.

I am sure they were in agony, but rather than whining and complaining about the cost of following Christ, they were singing. And you know what? I don't imagine this was a conscious plan. I don't think Paul said to Silas, "Look, let's praise God and then He'll send an earthquake to deliver us."

No.

I imagine that in a cracked, hurting voice, Paul asked, "Silas, how are you doing?" I can hear Silas just moan, and then maybe Paul said, "You know, Silas, the only thing that will improve this place is His presence. We need His presence."[13]

And as they praised God, He entered the scene.

He *always* does.

Prison chains fell off.

As they talked and sang to God, the other prisoners were listening.

It is the same with us. Others are watching to see how we handle this battle. They want answers. And they are hoping we have some.

Paul challenges us to endure hardship like good soldiers.[14] And doing that will require the determination to rise.

The determination to not quit.

Even when quitting is easier.

Winston Churchill captured the spirit of determination with his words:

> We shall not flag or fail.
> We shall fight to the end.
> We shall fight in France.
> We shall fight on the seas and oceans.
> We shall fight with growing confidence and growing strength
>   in the air.
> We shall defend our island whatever the cost may be.
> We shall fight on the beaches.
> We shall fight on the landing grounds.
> We shall fight in the streets.
> We shall fight in the hills.
> We shall never, never surrender.[15]

A few days after the cancer diagnosis, I remember crawling into my bed and crying and crying. Snot was running down my face. It was not pretty. *Would I make it through this?* I wondered. Then my husband put some great worship music on and crawled into bed with me. Together we cried and worshiped our God. (Okay, so I probably did not sound pretty either.) But in that moment I was rising on the inside.

On the outside, I appeared totally overwhelmed . . . but the warrior was rising on the inside.

I got up the next day and really began the battle. It soon became apparent to me that there were thousands of women who were watching to see how to get victory. Just as in the time of Paul and Silas, the prisoners were watching.

I did not have the option of lying down and quitting.

I had an obligation to rise.

I have it still.

So do you.

What battle are you in the middle of now? (If you are not in one right now, your turn is next week!)

Is it your marriage?

Well, there are those watching who need to see how to have a great one, so don't give up.

Please.

Is it raising children?

Well, there are those watching who need to see how to raise healthy ones, so don't give up.

Please.

Is it feeding the hungry?

Well, there are hungry people who need to be fed, so don't give up.

Please.

Is it coming out of an abusive relationship?

Well, there are those watching who need to see how to get out, too, so don't give up.

Please.

Is it overcoming depression?

Well, there are those watching who need to see how to do it, so don't give up.

Please.

chapter 3

stay at your post!

In 1776, the Revolutionary War was raging.

The young colonials fought valiantly, risking it all for freedom.

Most were not trained soldiers.

They were simply passionate about liberty.

One such colonial was stationed at his cannon during the battle of Fort Washington.

The sounds of war screamed.

Bullets and cannonballs exploded around him.

One of them found its mark and killed him.

His wife, Margaret Corbin, took over the manning of the cannon until she herself was wounded.

Thanks, Margaret, for staying at your post.

The trip across the Rocky Mountains in 1836 was beyond difficult—and she was the first woman to make it.

It was only because the mission was so clear in her heart that she could even bear it.

Along with her husband, Marcus, Narcissa was determined to bring the love of Jesus to the native tribe of Cayuse, an isolated people group located in modern-day Oregon.

While there, she endured hardships that most of us modern women couldn't imagine.

Her own two-year-old daughter died.

It certainly would have been easier to go back to the comfort of the East Coast. But instead she raised orphaned native and pioneer children, loving them as her own.

She continued to love the people she had been sent across the country to love.

In 1847 an epidemic of measles struck the area and caused so many deaths among the Cayuse that they suspected the Whitmans and other missionaries of using evil power against them. A handful of the Cayuse entered the Whitman home and killed Marcus and Narcissa. Some of her last words were: "Tell my sister that I died at my post."

I imagine there are people in heaven because Narcissa stayed at her post.

Most of you probably don't remember where you were at 4:30 A.M. on January 17, 1994.

I will never forget.

I was fast asleep in bed with my husband, Philip, when suddenly I was violently shaken.

I quickly realized that we were having a very large earthquake here in Southern California. The shaking was terrible and the noise was even worse.

It sounded as if a bomb were exploding under my house.

The alarm system was screeching.

I could hear all the wedding china (that I had spent hours picking out!) hitting the tile floor and shattering into a million pieces.

While the shaking was still going on, Philip yelled that he would go get Paris (our two-and-a-half-year-old daughter) and that I should get our son, Jordan (who was six at the time).

It was pitch black. Every light in the whole city was out. I couldn't even see my own hand in front of my face.

As I was stumbling across our bedroom to get to the hall, a dresser flew across the room and clipped me in the legs.

Now I was bleeding and crawling down the hall to get my son.

When I got to his door, it wouldn't open. Something was blocking it.

I was slightly freaked out!

But eventually we got it open and stood in the doorframe as the first aftershock hit.

We realized that we would need to get out of the house quickly.

We held each other as we made our way to the front lawn.

Eventually the sun came over the horizon and we could see the devastation.

Every wall of our house had either fallen or was cracked.

Most appliances had been destroyed.

This certainly hadn't been part of my plan for my life!

For weeks the earth under our home constantly moved. We experienced aftershock after aftershock. And we got very tired of our earth moving.

We decided we wanted to move to a place where the earth didn't move—like somewhere in the middle of the country!

It is embarrassing to admit that we visited different cities, looking for a new place to call home.

We didn't really tell anyone—we were too busy thinking of changing our post.

Thankfully, Philip and I came to our senses and stayed put. I actually cringe now to think of what we almost did. Not that there aren't great places in our country to plant a church—they just aren't great places for us.

Our post is Los Angeles . . . earthquakes and all!

Our church has grown by thousands since 1994. Hundreds have begun real relationships with God. We have had the opportunity to make a significant impact in our city by demonstrating what a multicultural, multigenerational church looks like. God is doing an amazing thing in our hometown.

And we almost abandoned our post.

Just so you know, I don't think it will necessarily be required of us to die at our post (whew!), but as warriors we will be required to *stay* at our post.

One of my posts is . . . *wife*. So, even if Philip and I have a serious disagreement (and come on, if you've been married longer than six weeks, you've had a serious disagreement!) *and* I am not a happy warrior *and* Mr. Universe walks by wearing a Speedo and quoting Shakespeare, I'm not distracted (at least not much ☺). Why not? Because I know that my post is next to Philip forever.

Marriage is not for the weak or the faint of heart.

It will require everything you have to make it work.

It will demand that you change, that you learn, that you adapt.

Two becoming one sounds a lot easier than it really is.

Two becoming one sounds so romantic.

Did you light the unity candle at your wedding? Or have you seen it done? There are three candles on display. The outside two are lit, one representing the life of the bride and other representing the life of the groom. The bride takes her candle and the groom takes his, and together they light the third, and larger, candle in the middle.

Thus, the two become one.

I just really wish it were that easy.

Marriage is more like each of you coming together with a box of parts. You each bring your box of parts: your past, your hurts, your personalities, your issues . . . and together you are going to build something amazing. It will just require serious work—and it is a lot harder than lighting the candle!

There are times when you won't be happy. (It is not your husband's job to make you happy, by the way. That would be your job.)

There are seasons in a marriage that might be harder than others.

There are times when your home might feel like a battlefield. (Let me just say, if it actually *is* a battlefield and you are being physically abused, please get yourself to a safe place and get help. I would not want anyone to stay in a situation that is dangerous. You both need help and most times it is better to get help separate from each other.)

There are times when you might wonder why you married him in the first place.

There are times when you might think that another man would be better at meeting your needs.

There are times when you might be convinced that you married the wrong person. (We have all felt this.)

There are times when it just might be boring. I have talked to so many couples over the years that have let their marriage enter the boring zone. All marriages have boring moments—sometimes life is boring, but our marriage shouldn't be for too long.

Here are some tips for staying at your marriage post . . .

- *Do your part in making the marriage interesting.* In fact, be an interesting person—have a passion, a hobby, or master a craft.

- *Love life.* That is a decision, not a feeling. People who love life are fun to be around. Smile even when it is hard. Happy feelings generally follow happy doings.

- *Don't be so needy.* The secret to being loved is not having to be loved—*having* to be loved puts all the focus on you, and neediness can be a real drain on a marriage.

- *Listen when he talks.* Really. Don't just be thinking of what else you need to do—be fully engaged. I know it is not always easy because sometimes it takes a *loooonnnnng* time for him to spit it out. It would have been quicker for me to finish his sentence. (I probably would have gotten the ending wrong, but it certainly would have been interesting!)

- *Be interested in sex.* Make that part of your relationship fun again. If it needs a boost, boost it! Give him a sultry look. Buy new lingerie. Don't let intimacy die.

Stay at your post.

Other soldiers are counting on it.

Another of my posts is . . . *mother*, so I spend time training my children and loving them, even though there are times I want to send them far, far away! Most of the time, I love being Mom.

But there are some moments when it is just *so* hard. (Can anyone relate?)

Sometimes correction is necessary—and sometimes giving it is emotionally exhausting.

I know women whose older children have gotten involved in everything from pornography, to driving without a license, to cutting school.

All of these require correction.

I am sure these women feel like they are in a battle.

They are.

Perhaps it would be easier for them to just throw up their hands in frustration, give up and emotionally withdraw from their children.

Many women do.

But these women do not.

They have stayed at their post.

Are you tempted to leave yours? Well, keep in mind these tips for staying at the mother post.

- Be grateful that you have a child. There are thousands of women who haven't been able to.

- Take a moment to focus on something good your children have done.

- Do something fun with your kids. Not homework or chores, but something that involves lots of laughter.

- Get together with other mothers who are committed to staying at the "mother post."

Another of my posts is . . . *teacher*, so I spend time training my mind, going to conferences and studying so that I can continually improve.

My style of teaching can be fun and inspiring, but not all see it that way (I know—what a shock!). Sometimes women, perhaps out of their own insecurity or because they just disagree with me, attack and criticize what I am doing.

They are the spectators.

In life, there are always more spectators than players. There are more people in the grandstands than there are players on the field—mainly because there is only one requirement to sit in the grandstand: being critical.

While we are in the stands, we all think *we* could have made that goal, shot that basket, given a more profound teaching or told a better story.

If we listen to too much criticism, we can find ourselves trying to second-guess the post to which we have been assigned.

I am open to correction from God and from a handful of people to whom I am accountable. I just have to ignore spiteful criticism from others, or I find myself doubting the purpose of my life, wondering if I do have anything good to offer my generation.

Being in front of people makes me easy to shoot at, so I think, *I don't want to be target practice for others. Maybe I should give up on the woman thing and become a professional bowler* (not a chance, by the way!) *or just sit in the back of church, where I can't feel the arrows.*

But even though sometimes it might be tempting, I cannot abandon my post.

And staying at the teacher post requires that I work. That I am disciplined enough to take time to study and prepare. Some might think that I just stand on the platform and words just pour out of my mouth. Not quite that easy. I have put hours into preparing that message.

When those hours get tough to find, I remind myself why I need to persevere. I remember my very own tips for staying at the job post.

- Know that it is more than a job . . . it is a calling. It is easy to abandon a job. It's much harder to walk away from a calling.

- Get training continually. The more training, the more equipped and the more capable you will be.

- Increase your capacity. We should be able to handle more this year than last year.

- Be accountable to people who can help you. Get input from others who are perhaps farther down the road than you are.

- Become skilled at gracefully handling both criticism and praise.

Another of my posts is . . . *friend*, so I invest time in people, even perhaps when I'd rather be alone.

Or even when a particular friend is being particularly annoying!

I love cards.

I love giving cards.

I love receiving cards.

I love going to the card store and standing around reading them.

Most of the time, however, I have found that some of the sentimental dribble on the cards is just that . . . sentimental dribble—albeit beautifully composed sentimental dribble!

Building a friendship and remaining a faithful friend take almost as much work as building and maintaining a marriage.

Why?

Because we are different. Each of us is unique.

So when the "unique beauty" of your friend is beginning to wear a bit, keep in mind these tips for staying at the friend post.

- Be patient with the differences.
- Forgive.
- Be happy when she gets a promotion. Even if you didn't get one.
- Send a card.
- Let her cry—and cry with her.
- See chapter 6 in this book.

My main post is . . . *believer*.

In the midst of the battle, can I still believe in the goodness of God? When enemies surround me, can I still worship my God? Or do I blame Him? Can I remain a faithful believer?

Jehoshaphat, king of Judah, was surrounded by a bunch of "ites" (Moabites, Ammonites, Meunites, Pain-in-the-ites) who all wanted to destroy him. I imagine it was terrifying.

Perhaps his life flashed before him.

But he did an amazing thing.

He didn't get angry with God.

He didn't ask why.

Before they planned to march into battle, he bowed down and worshiped God. He then appointed a choir for God that was to march ahead of the troops.

A choir.

The praise team.

He didn't put the guys with the swords in front.

He put the worship leaders out there to lead the charge.

The choir sang, "Give thanks to God, His love never quits."[1]

Guess he was serious about his post as a believer . . . as a worshiper.

While they worshiped, God set ambushes and the enemies were destroyed.

Can you remain a believer in the midst of your battle?

Leslie is a friend of mine.

She lives on the East Coast with her husband and two young children.

They are pastors and are working hard at reaching people with the love of Jesus.

I met her almost seven years ago when she came to a conference to hear me teach. After the conference, we had a great day laughing and shopping (let's hear it for girl time!).

We connected by phone and email over the next few years. She mentioned an illness she was fighting. The name of the disease didn't really register with me. At one point she emailed and said that she was having difficulty talking and so emailing was easier for her.

In our email correspondence, she would ask questions about church leadership, running a women's ministry, or just life as a twenty-first-century woman. She was always upbeat, curious, confident and full of faith. I forgot about whatever disease she was dealing with, because she seemed so positive about life.

Then an email came that gave me the impression that she was just a bit discouraged. This was a bit unusual, so I asked her just what the disease was that she was facing. When she told me it was ALS, more commonly known as Lou Gehrig's disease, I was stunned. After learning about the illness and how it ravages the body, I asked her what part of her body was still functional. She said, "My eyes." She used her eyes to communicate the alphabet.

Her eyes.

That's it.

And I had had no idea.

When I went to see her, I saw the reality of what it means to stay at the post of believer.

She can't talk to a girlfriend on the phone.

She can't go out to dinner.

She can't hold her children.

She can't kiss her husband.

She can't move.

And yet . . . she loves God.

She sees Him as good.

From her chair/bed, and using only her eyes, she leads the women's ministry at her church. She plans events. She strategizes about the future of the Church.

She loves.

She worships.

She believes.

She is staying at her post.

I am in awe.

Could I do that?

I wonder.

Susan B. Anthony was ridiculed and persecuted simply because she thought every human being ought to be treated with dignity. She encountered threats of physical violence and cruel crowds. In 1856, the townspeople of Syracuse hanged her in effigy and then dragged her image through the streets. Still, in 1863, Susan helped to organize a Women's National Loyal League to support and petition for the Thirteenth Amendment, which would outlaw slavery.

And it passed.

She then began to campaign for full citizenship for both African Americans and women, including the right to vote, in the Fourteenth and Fifteenth Amendments. I am sure she was disappointed when the rights of women were not included in either of those amendments.

But she did not give up.

Storms were brewing all around her and she remained at her post.

She persevered in spite of huge obstacles. I am sure at times she grew weary, but I am also sure that the end result was always more important than her momentary discomfort.

Thank you, Susan, for staying at your post!

Another legendary woman who stayed at her post . . .

Her life was not easy.

She was born into slavery in 1820 and suffered greatly at the hands of her owners.

In 1850, she escaped into Canada, but she didn't rest there.

From 1851 until the end of the Civil War, she helped rescue more than 300 slaves, whom she brought to safety in Canada.

Time and time again, she herself went back into the South, risking capture and certain death every time.

Because she wanted as many people freed as possible.

Countless numbers owe their lives to her.

Thank you, Harriet Tubman, for staying at your post.

And yet another . . .

She graduated first in her class and underwent surgery that restored some of her sight.

In 1887, she moved to Alabama to become the teacher and caretaker of a deaf-blind child.

The child was Helen Keller, and the woman who stayed at her post through the battle was Anne Sullivan.

Through Anne's creativity, discipline, persistence and patience, she was able to reach and then ultimately teach Helen.

Against all odds, Helen eventually attended Radcliffe College and graduated with honors.

As Helen's teacher, Anne pioneered techniques of education for the handicapped and lobbied for increased opportunities for those without sight.

Because of Anne's teaching success, Helen's life became an inspiration for many.

Thank you, Anne, for staying at your post.

The apostle Paul was awaiting his execution in prison when he wrote some powerful words to his protégé, Timothy. In his final letter, he offered wisdom about the Church, life and the future. And he cast one last look over his shoulder, summarizing his life: "I have fought the good fight, I have finished the race, I have kept the faith."[2]

Basically he was saying that he had stayed at his post.

Paul was a great man.

Whole cities of people came to know God because of him.

He introduced the continent of Europe to the love of Jesus.

Paul wrote half of the New Testament.

His secret to greatness wasn't in his knowledge, though—and he was a knowledgeable guy.

It wasn't in his looks.

It wasn't because of his eloquence.

Paul was extraordinary because he did not quit. He stayed at his post.

After his conversion on the road to Damascus, Paul found the people around him hostile; they despised and mocked him. He could have said, "There is no love here. I'm throwing in the towel."

But he didn't.

Then the Christians didn't believe his conversion. Even the Christian leaders doubted him.

And the Jews tried to kill him.

He was thrown into prison.

More than once.

He was involved in a shipwreck.

He endured a vicious stoning at the hands of a cruel crowd that left him for dead. How did he respond? He got up and returned to the city that was filled with the very people who had just tried to kill him!

Just like the Energizer bunny, he kept going and going and going!

He stayed at his post.

Like Paul, you and I will have plenty of opportunities to quit. Lots of distractions beckoning to us. Lots of pathways leading away from our post.

We can't take them.

No matter how hard the journey is.

No matter how tough the battle.

Have any of us ever felt like quitting?

Sure.

Most of us do at one point or another. And maybe there are a few things we should quit, like our diet of doughnuts and fried everything or a 10-pack-a-day cigarette habit. But sometimes we give up things we need to keep working on: a marriage, a career, a weight-loss goal, an idea.

During the 1968 Mexico City Olympics, a marathon runner from Tanzania came into the arena headed for the finish line—a full hour after the winner had been announced. He was bloodied, hurt and bandaged. A reporter asked the question, "Why didn't you quit? The winner came in hours ago and you are hurt." The runner said, "My country did not send me to start the race, they sent me to finish it."[3]

The same is true of us.

We have been sent to finish.

In a marathon, the photographers are at the finish line.

Not at mile eight.

Jesus is waiting to say "Well done" at our finish line.

We cannot abandon the posts we have been assigned to. A whole generation of people need the baton we will hand them. They need the wisdom we will gain from staying at our post. I am aware that this might be a new thought—that not everybody in today's culture thinks of the generation to come. But you and I are different. We are warriors.

They used to shoot deserters.

Now they just prosecute them.

Regardless, being AWOL (absent without leave) is not good.

It is a serious offense.

We have some posts to which we have been assigned.

Let's stay there.

I actually think it is very selfish of us to give up in the tough times. I know there are people we are supposed to help—people who are just on the other side of this battle.

Those people have to be our priority.

On September 11, 2001, Flight 93 crashed in an isolated field in Pennsylvania.

The passengers on that flight were willing to endure—to stay at their post for the sake of others. They made a decision in the middle of their battle that saved countless lives.

Jesus stayed at His post, the Bible tells us, "for the joy set before him."[4]

He did not quit.

He completed His journey because He saw us, you and me, in His future.

We are the joy that was set before Him.

He stayed at His post . . . for us.

I don't know to which posts you have been assigned.

Maybe you are a student. Finish that class. Stay at that post.

How about your job? Can you remain faithful to that post?

Do you have a goal? A mission? A vision? Stay at your post.

I am doing my best to stay at the posts to which I have been assigned.

How about you?

> <u>People are watching us as we stay at our post,</u>
> *alertly, unswervingly . . .*
> *in hard times, tough times, bad times;*
> *when we're beaten up, jailed, and mobbed;*
> *working hard, working late, working without eating;*
> *with pure heart, clear head, steady hand;*
> *in gentleness, holiness, and honest love;*
> *when we're telling the truth, and when God's showing his power;*
> *when we're doing our best setting things right;*
> *when we're praised, and when we're blamed;*
> *slandered, and honored; true to our word, though distrusted;*
> *ignored by the world, but recognized by God;*
> *terrifically alive, though rumored to be dead;*
> *beaten within an inch of our lives, but refusing to die;*
> *immersed in tears, yet always filled with deep joy;*
> *living on handouts, yet enriching many;*
> *having nothing, having it all.*
>
> 2 Corinthians 6:3-10

chapter 4

focus!

She was on her way to the swings.

Her two-year-old legs were walking as fast as they could.

"Oh, what's that?"

Ah, she notices the butterfly . . . and starts to chase it.

"Oh, what's that?"

She sees a piece of gum stuck to the sidewalk and tries to "unstuck" it. Yuck.

While sitting down, she sees ants all in a row and wants to watch where they are going.

The swings have been forgotten.

Her focus lost.

Too much to see along the way.

This might be acceptable and even cute in a toddler. But as we grow older, yielding to distractions has a price.

She was on her way to a diploma.

She was taking all the right classes.

"Oh, man, is he cute!"

She notices the guy.

She can study another time, but right now there is a party to go to.

Another party.

A trip to the beach.

Guess she better drop that class—it is too much work.

So is that one.

She has lost her focus.

At least she has a boyfriend.

Too bad about the diploma.

Maybe one day.

She was on the journey to a healthy body.

She was beginning to eat the right foods.

She was even exercising.

"Oh, what a hard day at work," she says. "I deserve a treat."

She eats a cookie.

She eats the whole bag.

"Today was exhausting. I will exercise tomorrow."

Tomorrow comes.

She is still too tired.

Her focus shifted from a healthy body to her bad day.

So much for the new outfit she wanted to wear. It still does not fit.

Maybe one day.

She was building a marriage.

They smiled at each other in the mornings.

They cuddled at night.

"Oh, man, being a working mom sure is exhausting. Go ahead, honey, go to the movie without me . . . I am just too tired."

She went to her daughter's play.

She helped with her son's homework.

"Sorry, honey, I am just too tired to make love."

She got a promotion at work.

Hard to keep focused on her marriage.

"Sorry, honey, I don't have time to take a vacation."

Maybe one day.

She had lost her focus—now she might lose her marriage.

She felt God whisper to her heart—He had children who were hurting in Africa.

She was to help come up with an idea for how to take care of the orphans.

"Oh, wow, this is a lot of work."

"There are just so many children that need help."

Someone told her that it was too big of a job for her to do.

Even governments couldn't do it.

She listened.

"Maybe I can do something when I have more time."

Maybe one day.

She forgot His whisper.

She lost her focus.

As warriors, any battle that you and I are going to win will require focus. Every day the stuff of life competes for our focus.

For the Marine, boot camp is a time of great focus and little freedom. Still, the human capacity for distraction cannot be completely
eradicated. Even under the watchful eye of a drill instructor, one's
mind can, and will, wander.

But drill instructors are ready for this. If they begin to feel the focus
of the group slip, they simply bark the word "Eyeballs!" to which
every recruit will instinctively respond by focusing their eye on their
leader and yelling "Click!" Now "click" may seem a strange
response, but the sound of 80 voices shouting the word "click" will
refocus the most lethargic of minds.[1]

Must be nice to have a built-in safety against distraction.

Wouldn't it be great if, at any time we were headed off course,
someone would yell "Eyeballs," thus focusing our attention back
on the present moment.

Too bad there is no pocket-sized drill instructor for us to carry
through life.

All that we will accomplish in life flows out of our present.

We can dream about the future and remember the past
but we control only the present.

Yet rarely do we live in it.

In our minds, we live mostly for better times. Whether lost
in memories or consumed by dreams, our thoughts are
often on the experiences of another day.

Some float through life thinking only of tomorrow.

One day they'll be rich.

Get back in shape.

Paint the kitchen.

Help the homeless.

See Europe.

One day.

My calendar lists every official day including Virgin of Guadalupe Day, Administrative Professional Day, and Sweetest Day (by the way, it falls on a Saturday this year so plan accordingly) but I don't see any days labeled "One Day." Like Linus' Great Pumpkin, year after year, it never seems to come.[2]

"One day when I have more time . . ."

"One day when the kids are gone . . ."

"One day when we have more money . . ."

Our "one days" are determined by our todays.

You and I are to live *in* this moment *for* the future. We can't live *for* the moment because then we are too easily distracted and will mess up our future. We can't be distracted by the gum stuck to the sidewalk, the cute boy in class or the cookies on the grocery store shelf. Our future depends on it.

A person focused in the present exercises *today*.

Signs up for classes *today*.

Eats healthy *today*.

Writes the business plan *today*.

This person knows that, each day she holds in her hand the seeds for tomorrow. But if she doesn't kneel down, dig a hole and plant them, they will remain seeds.

Every great sports movie has a locker room speech. When the chips are down, the coach will turn the tide with one brilliant, soul stirring appeal. Whether he's telling them to "be perfect" or "win one for the Gipper," all of these speeches have the same basic goal. They help the players shake off the mental dust of distraction and focus them on the importance of the next few minutes of their life. It's an "Eyeballs" moment.

In the movie *Braveheart*, Mel Gibson, portraying the Scottish hero William Wallace, gives a scattering army the courage to reassemble and win, by reminding them that the quality of the rest of their lives will be determined by what they are about to do. They were focused on walking away so they could live another day. His speech helped them see that *today*, was the time for living. I could almost hear them yell "Click."[3]

Even in the middle of a battle we must make tough decisions that will affect our future. I read somewhere that if a 21-year-old saved $100 a month, with compound interest, she would have $1 million by the time she was 60. Sounds easy, but most of us can't do it—because something always comes along to make us lose focus. We want the million down the road, but today we want those new shoes or that DVD, so we don't save and we don't reach our goal. You and I cannot allow the battle we are in to cause us to lose sight of our goal. We must keep our focus.

Many times juvenile prisoners lose their focus—they forget that their goal is to get out of jail as soon as possible. They get distracted from the goal of parole, of getting out of prison, and so they make stupid decisions just 30 days before they are up for parole.

Thirty days.

They could be free in 30 days.

But instead they start a fight, hurt another prisoner or attack a guard. Or they just decide to break a rule.

Their prison stay just got longer.

Why?

Because they lost focus.

The apostle Paul was arrested for teaching about Jesus.

Because Paul was a Roman citizen, he appealed to Caesar and so was sent to Rome.

He boarded a prison ship.

While the ship was in the middle of the sea, a storm arose.

The waves were massive, the rain relentless and the wind fierce.

In the middle of the storm, some of the sailors forgot their goal of reaching Rome.

They took their eyes off the target and looked at the waves.

If Paul hadn't been on board making good decisions, all might have been lost.

Jesus visited His disciples one time by walking on the water.

Peter thought that was pretty cool, so he asked Jesus if he could do it too.

Jesus said, "Come on, Peter."

Peter stepped out of the boat—and walked toward Jesus.

He was doing fine until he took his eyes off Jesus and focused on the waves.

Is it any easier to walk on the water when the ocean is calm than when it is full of waves?

I don't think so.

Louis Pasteur continued to work on vaccines during the month that his two daughters died from one of the diseases he was trying to prevent.

He suffered a brain hemorrhage that affected the left side of his body. He continued his study.[4]

Focus.

Rumor has it that Michelangelo continued his work on the Sistine Chapel in spite of excruciating back pain (after all, he painted the whole thing lying on his back!).

He forgot to eat.

He didn't get much sleep.

He didn't change clothes.

In fact, when he finally took his socks off, his skin came off with them. Gross.

Focus.

If we are going to make it through battles, we have to remember our focus.

If you are in a rough spot in your marriage, you have to remember that your goal is to build a strong marriage. I have known so many couples that have faced serious storms in their marriage.

Some lost sight of the goal. Because the marriage was in a tough place, they began to shift their focus toward work. Spending hours at work seemed easier than dealing with the challenge of their marriage. The more time they spent away from their spouse, the more the marriage disintegrated.

Most of us have been in a financial battle at one time or another. If we are going to win this one, we must learn to live within a budget. I hate that part! I wasn't really raised with the concept of a budget. If I wanted money, I just asked my dad for it (I know, you're thinking, *Spoiled brat!*).

When I married Philip, however, things changed. Sometimes he said I couldn't buy something because it wasn't in our budget. The first time he said that, I cried, because I thought we must be poor.

"No," he assured me, "we have a budget so that we won't be poor."

It still took me a while to get it.

Stay focused.

Stick to the budget.

Sometimes we make decisions based on our emotions—and that can lead to a serious mess.

Our church has so many wonderfully creative people. I love that!
I love the actors, dancers, singers, television producers . . . all of
them. They have made our church fun, creative and energetic. Like
most of us, however, they could find their strength to be their weakness if they are not careful. It is their ability to tap into their emotions that helps them write amazing songs, feel the characters they
portray and dance with passion. But anyone who lets her emotions
lead her discovers she is on her way to a mess!

I am grateful that I have emotions.

That I can feel.

But emotions can work for us or against us.

So I can't be led by them.

We can't pay our bills when we "feel" like it.

Nope.

We have to pay them when they are due.

We can't just show up to work when we want.

No.

We must show up when we are expected to.

We can't just spend time with our kids or demonstrate love for our
husband when it sounds like fun.

No.

We must do those things regardless.

Sometimes we lose our focus because we just have too much on
our mind.

The computer geeks (and I use that term very respectfully!) that I
have known say that often our computer crashes because we are
running too many programs at once.

When we are in a battle, sometimes we try to do too many things rather than focus on the one thing that will get us through.

There are a lot of "good" things we might be able to do, but often "good" is the enemy of "best."

Sometimes we lose our focus because of temptation.

And we can be tempted by so many things: food, gossip, men.

I knew of a marriage that was in the midst of a storm.

The wife became distracted by another man.

She wasn't a bad person.

She just stopped concentrating on her marriage.

Perhaps she lost hope, got tired of working on it.

Understandable.

Only now, she has an even bigger battle to deal with.

We can lose our focus because of a series of disappointments.

Life is full of them, and some of us handle them better than others. Maybe you have faced various rejections at job interviews—talk about disappointing!

You can respond in a number of ways.

You can get angry and hate all employers.

You can sit on the street corner and beg for money.

You can take a class.

You can make an effort to become more desirable in the eyes of employers.

You can keep applying for jobs.

Warriors can't focus on the disappointment; we have to keep our eyes fixed on where we want to go.

Recently, I heard a radio show psychologist challenge a caller. The caller was a fairly new mom whose husband was in the military and stationed in the Far East. She was asking the psychologist how to deal with the depression she was feeling. She missed her husband—and her husband was missing so much of his daughter's life.

The first thing the doctor did was challenge where the woman's focus was. She got her to look at all the great things in her life. After all, didn't she have the freedom to go out to lunch where she wanted, visit a friend or watch what she wanted on television? Instead of focusing on what she was lacking, she needed to be focusing on what she had. Then the doctor told her she needed to be thinking of her husband, who was dealing with his own loneliness and fear. He certainly did not need to be worrying about her. So maybe she needed to take her eyes off herself for a moment. Maybe she should be filming her daughter every day and sending the video to him. Or writing notes in a journal for him daily. Or getting together with other military wives. The doctor agreed that yes, her situation was sad, but it could be livable if she would shift her focus.

I liked that.

Sometimes our problems come because we spend so much time navel gazing.

"My issues . . ."

"My hurts . . ."

"My lacks . . ."

Maybe we should all go spend a month in a developing nation. I bet our focus would shift.

Sometimes we can just lose focus when it comes to our destiny.

Which is the "why" behind what we do.

Paul's destiny included going to Rome.

I am sure he kept that in mind as the waves were crashing against the ship.

There will be waves crashing against your ship, too. Can you keep your Rome in sight?

Occasionally we can lose focus because we are so preoccupied with what we need that we have forgotten what God has done for us so far.

One day Jesus was talking with His disciples. They were a little panicked because they had traveled to the other side of the sea and had forgotten to bring bread. They wondered how they were going to eat. I can just see Jesus shaking His head as He asked, "Why are you worried about the bread? Don't you remember that we fed 5,000 with just 2 loaves and 5 fish? Maybe you can tell me how many leftovers there were."

I can just hear the disciples saying, very quietly, "Um, 12 baskets full."

Jesus said, "I can't hear you—how many were there?"

Perhaps the disciples were a little embarrassed then, as they answered a little louder, "Twelve."

Jesus continued, "And if I'm not mistaken, we recently fed 4,000 men with just 7 loaves and a few fish. How many baskets were left over then?"

The disciples probably replied very sheepishly, "Seven."

Jesus asked, "What was that?"

The disciples replied a little louder, "Seven large baskets of leftovers."[5]

Was Jesus trying to embarrass them? No.

He was sharpening their focus. Were they going to study and worry about the need before them and panic, or were they going to remember the provision Jesus had always made for them?

A warrior focuses on what she is going *to* . . . not what she is going *through*.

On my journey toward my goal of getting a black belt in karate, I had to learn to break boards (it's a great way to work off frustration and much safer than breaking someone's head!). Breaking boards has little to do with strength and everything to do with focus. I have seen little girls smash through a board effortlessly, while brawny men hurt their hand. I learned that in order to split the board, I had to focus on a spot beyond the piece of wood—not on the board itself. If I focused on the board, my hand might just stop at the board and not break through.

It took everything within me to not let the cancer knock me off course. The treatments were sometimes painful, sometimes time consuming and always annoying. My purpose, the goal of my life, didn't change just because I was in a battle. I had to continue to look toward where I was headed, even to a point past my own health, to the generation of women I have been assigned to reach. The pain certainly tried to be a distraction—and some days it was. But overall I tried really hard not to let my circumstances cause me to lose sight of my own Rome.

The writer of Hebrews challenged us to look away from all that will distract and keep looking to Jesus, who is the leader and source of our faith. Jesus was able to endure the cross, not by dwelling on the nails and the betrayal, but by focusing on the joy before Him. He kept His mind focused on the fact that He would ultimately be sitting at the right hand of the Father—and that once again, hurting people could have a loving relationship with their Creator. He focused on the victory, not the challenge.

How about you?

the baton exchange

She was born in 1910.

At 12 she joined an abbey.

At 18 she became a nun.

In 1950 she started the Missionaries of Charity in Calcutta, India, with 12 other nuns.

She loved the poor.

She fed the hungry.

She held orphans.

She showed mercy to the dying.

In 1973 she received the Nobel Peace Prize.

She was consistently found by the Gallup Poll to be the world's most admired person.

By the time of her death in 1997, the Missionaries of Charity had over 4,000 sisters, an associated brotherhood of 300 members and over 100,000 lay volunteers operating 610 missions in 123 countries.

The duty of caring for hurting people did not die when Mother Teresa did.

No.

She had spent years training a new generation of women.

She was prepared for the baton exchange.

The condition of women in the 1800s in the U.S. wasn't great.

We had no rights whatsoever.

For more than 45 years, she championed the cause of women.

She fought tirelessly to give women the right to vote, the right to have a say in our future.

She traveled constantly giving speeches . . . often to hostile crowds.

At one point in New York, her image was hung in effigy and dragged through the streets.

She began to see that the amendment that would give women the vote might not come in her lifetime, so in the 1880s, when she was in her 60s, she began to train a new generation of suffragists.

She realized at one point that she wasn't doing it for herself but for the daughters to come.

She died in 1906, and the amendment that gave women the vote did not pass until 1920.

So she didn't see victory in her lifetime.

But I guarantee you.

She saw it.

She said that she was honored to have helped begin the movement and that she would entrust the finishing of the battle to a new generation.

Once again, thank you, Susan B. Anthony.

Thanks for not bungling the baton exchange.

I have read the Bible through a number of times. And have read the book of Titus many times. However, there was a moment a few years ago when chapter two jumped out at me. Basically it is challenging the older woman to assume responsibility for the younger woman. I thought, "Great, when I get to be 103, then I will be the older woman, and I will train up all those younguns!"

I heard a whisper from heaven, "Holly, is there anyone younger than you on the planet?"

I had to think for a minute.

After all, I am *not* old . . . so I must be young!

But really, of course, there is someone younger than me on the earth.

As soon as I admitted that, then I heard heaven again, "Well, Holly, you are an older woman. As long as there is someone younger than you alive and kicking, then you are an older woman."

Wasn't sure I really wanted to be called an old woman.

In a sick way, it makes me feel better to call you an old woman too.

And you are.

You are an old woman.

Why?

Because right now, in your world, there is a woman younger than you are.

If you are 16, you are an old woman.

Why?

Because there are 10-year-olds who need to learn from you.

If you are 25, you are an old woman.

Why?

Because that 16-year-old needs to know what you know.

If you are 43, you are an old woman.

Why?

Because there is a 20-something who desperately needs to learn from you.

If you are 99, you got all of us!

As long as there is someone younger than you on the planet, you are an older woman. And as the older women, we do have a responsibility. We are to equip, motivate, inspire and train younger women.

Unlike volleyball and basketball, most track and field events are predominantly individual endeavors. One of the exceptions is the relay race.

I loved running in relay races. Why? Because, while I had to do my best to run my lap with commitment and endurance, whether we won the race was not entirely up to me.

Of course, I was aware that my performance could help my team or it could cost us the race. I was entirely responsible for the lap of the race I was running and so I spent months training for my lap. I could not blame anyone else for my performance. This lap was mine. If I tripped, stepped out of the lane or got a cramp, the fault was mine alone.

However, I found that most relay races are not won or lost in the individual laps, but rather in the baton exchange.

There are four runners in a relay race.

One starts with the baton, and one will carry it over the finish line.

As a runner is coming down the track, she is focused on one thing.

The runner to whom she will hand the baton.

She is looking for her and her outstretched hand.

The runner waiting for the baton is running in place.

And then at a given moment, she takes off.

Not quite full speed, but definitely moving.

She is no longer looking at the runner coming toward her with the baton—she is facing forward and her hand is reaching behind her. It is the job of the first runner to place the baton in the outstretched hand of the second runner. Once the baton is in the new runner's hand, she then takes off at full speed. The first runner, however, does not just stop on a dime. No, she continues running behind the second runner and slowly comes to a stop, keeping her eyes on her teammate.

Races are won and lost in the baton exchange.

Just ask the 2004 U.S. Olympic women's 4x100-meter relay team.

This women's relay team was focused and very fast.

Experts said that if they even just showed up to the finals, they would probably walk away with the gold.

They were that good.

They had easily won their first heat and had soundly defeated their opponents in the semifinal.

They were making it look easy.

But in the final round, the unthinkable happened.

Marion Jones failed to complete the pass to Lauren Williams. It's unclear what went wrong in that race. Williams suggested that maybe she had started running a bit too early. Jones was clearly tired from her participation in the long jump event earlier and had broken form by the end of her leg in the race. The two badly missed the pass a couple of times, slowed to a near stop and then went beyond the end of the passing zone for a disqualification from the race.

Jones said that miscommunication was the reason for the team's failure.

"I thought Angela [the first runner] ran a good leg and I thought I ran a good leg," said Jones.

"I just couldn't get the baton to Lauren, it didn't happen."

"I kept yelling, 'wait, stop, hold up' but after running 100 meters I was out of breath and I don't know if she could hear me."[1]

Not good.

They did not go to Athens to get disqualified.

Because of a missed baton pass, the race was lost.

Because the race was lost, the gold medal was lost—and for these two athletes, perhaps lost forever.

Christianity is a relay race. There are legends of faith that have gone before us. Centuries of baton passing have kept the faith alive. Your lap is important, but truly it is all about the baton. It is all about the message of hope, life and truth being passed to a new generation.

Warriors are continually looking for and training new recruits— because we realize there *are* future battles that need to be fought and won . . . and we may not be around for them.

Some of you reading this might be single moms who raised your children to be responsible adults (pretty awesome accomplishment!).

Well, I can guarantee you that right now, in your world, there is a younger single mom who is freaking out.

She does not know what to do.

She does not know how to manage her life.

She is worried about her children's future.

She needs to know what you know.

Maybe some of you were in debt at one point in your life.

Maybe you were on government aid and food stamps.

And maybe now you own your own home and have a savings account. Well, I would imagine there is a younger woman in your world who is panicking because of her financial situation.

She does not know how she will make ends meet.

She needs to know what you know.

Perhaps you have been married for 25 years (almost a miracle in my city!).

Somehow you built a marriage that is thriving.

I would bet that there is a young woman in your world who is considering a divorce.

She just can't figure out her husband and isn't sure what to do.

She needs to know what you know.

Maybe you graduated high school, went to college and persevered to complete a master's degree.

You have a job you love and feel fulfilled.

Right now, in your world, there is a young woman who is thinking of quitting school.

She just doesn't see the purpose.

She needs to know what you know.

Maybe you successfully navigated puberty *and* menopause.

Yeah!

There is certainly a younger woman in your life who is in the middle of one or the other. (And really, she doesn't want to learn about either from a man.)

She needs to know what you know.

Maybe you were once overweight.

You dealt with the issues of your heart, learned about the value of good nutrition and exercise, and lost the weight.

I would imagine that in your world right now is a young woman who is seriously overweight and is risking her future as a result.

She needs to know what you know.

Perhaps you came out of an abusive relationship.

Maybe you were raped.

You got help and feel stronger today than ever before.

I promise you, there is a younger woman in your world who is frightened.

She is ashamed.

She does not see a way out.

She needs to know what you know.

Maybe you were diagnosed with cancer.

Today you are healthy and unafraid.

What did you do?

There are numerous younger women who are waiting for answers.

They need to know what you know.

Dear Holly,

My name is Ruth and I am from Norfolk, England. I am 37 and am married to a mighty man of God who loves me. I have two brilliant kids. (How blessed am I?)

I was given Daily Steps for God Chicks *by a friend. While reading it, I felt so inspired by your courage to reach out and be the love of Christ while undergoing cancer treatment. Not only that, but to keep your focus on Jesus while dealing with all the other junk life throws. I thought, Boy, if I ever get ill, I hope I'll carry God in me like Holly.*

Well on day 64 of reading the book, I found a lump in my breast . . .

On Day 80, I found out that it was possibly not a good lump.

On day 81, I found out it was cancer.

Praise God that I feel equipped and ready for what lies ahead . . . and I know my wonderful God will be glorified!

Holly, I really want to encourage you. Don't lose heart. You must have bummer days, but I am inspired to remind you that all of this is so worth it. You are an awesome role model and a ground-breaker, and I know that hurts because breaking through is the hardest part. Press on . . . . you can do this.

You go, Girl!

Blessings with pom poms!

Love,

Ruth X

I received so many encouraging emails this past year. Many were from women who were in their own cancer battle. I included this email from Ruth (with her permission) not to say "Aren't I amazing?" but rather to make the point that each of us, at any given moment, has an obligation to pass on what we know so that younger runners will be equipped.

The younger women in your world are waiting for the baton.

Don't drop it.

Don't hang on to it.

Pass it on.

Another thought.

At any and every moment you are an older woman *and* a younger woman. You are being handed one baton and passing another off.

When in younger-woman mode, we are in the position of receiving. Most of the time we need to "shutteth uppeth!" We are looking for the baton—the wisdom, the insight, the help. So we probably need to be quiet and listen. I admit, I have been guilty when in younger-woman mode of doing all the talking!

Not smart.

Sometimes we try to make excuses, defend our position or explain away our lack of knowledge.

Stop it.

We need to humble ourselves so that we can learn.

> We shall some day be heeded and will think it was always so, just exactly as many young people think that all the privileges, all the freedom, all the enjoyments which woman now possesses always were hers. They have no idea of how every single inch of ground that she stands upon today has been gained by the hard work of some little handful of women in the past.
>
> Susan B. Anthony[2]

A baton exchange is coming.

Are you prepared?

Are you ready to receive one?

Are you ready to hand one off?

chapter 6

never alone

Now, gather yourself in troops, O daughter of troops;
a state of siege has been placed against us.
Micah 5:1, *AMP*

She was a teenager.

She had had an encounter beyond any she had known before.

She had seen an angel and now new life was growing within her.

Lots of people didn't believe.

She was the object of ridicule and scorn.

She needed help.

Just someone who could relate.

Someone who would understand.

She went to see her cousin.

And thankfully, Elizabeth did understand.

Now she didn't feel so alone anymore.

Mary learned that life is always better when done together.

The battle was intense.

The outcome seemed uncertain.

As long as Moses held his hands toward heaven, Joshua and the army were victorious.

But Moses was getting tired.

He felt the burden of his responsibility to keep his hands in the air.

How was he going to do it?

His arms were aching.

Wait.

He was not alone.

Aaron and Hur came to hold his arms up.

Together they saw the children of Israel get victory.

They had seen Him do miracles.

He healed the lame.

He opened blind eyes.

Now He told them to go and do the same.

It was exciting.

It was scary.

They had never done this by themselves.

Wait.

They weren't going alone.

He sent them in pairs.

Together.

Together is a big deal to God. We have not been created to function at our best in isolation. We have been designed to function as a part of something bigger.

We were created for team.

Family.

Community.

We have got to get good at this, but working together is definitely not easy.

Why?

Because people are weird. People can be hard to get along with. They don't do things your way. They don't see things your way. And yet, God asks us to love each other. To work together as a body.

There are some great elite fighting forces on the earth: the Navy SEALS, Marine Force Recon, Army Green Berets, British SAS— to name just a few. Members of these fighting forces are rarely deployed alone.

They work together as a unit.

The SEALS are often sent out in an eight-man platoon. Part of the SEAL code involves displaying loyalty to the team and teammates. They are trained to take responsibility for their own actions and the actions of their teammates.

Each member of the platoon has a different role to play within the unit. Each has a different skill and must learn to trust and rely on the others in order to fulfill his role. I doubt Navy SEALs argue over who should be the medic or who should handle the communication gear. I can't imagine one of them saying, "Hey, it's my turn to be the sniper!" No. They operate on the very correct assumption that the unique strengths of each member cause the unit to be stronger.

I was just thinking.

You and I have been deployed to the planet Earth in a platoon made up of over 1 billion teammates. We have a mission to fulfill, so we have to get good at working together. We each have different gifts, abilities and talents in order to fulfill our purpose. The apostle Paul said it like this: "Each person is given something to do that shows who God is: Everyone gets in on it, everyone benefits."[1]

One day a few winters ago I found myself on a ski lift with my son and one of his friends. (My first mistake!)

They like the black-diamond runs, and the truth is, I am not a black-diamond skier. I am more of a "casually make my way down the hill so I can go get a cup of hot chocolate" skier.

We got off the lift and quickly took off over a ledge. (Next mistake!)

When I landed on the other side, I soon realized that I was in serious trouble.

This particular ski run hadn't gotten a lot of snow, so bushes and trees were peeking through.

Not to mention that it was an almost vertical drop. (Okay, not exactly vertical . . . but close enough!)

My son and his friend were about a quarter of the way down when I screamed.

I was sure it was going to be my last day on Earth.

Jordan stopped and looked back at his crazy mother.

I told him (trying not to cry) that there was no way I was going to make it down the hill. He and his friend climbed back up to me (no easy task), and we tried to figure out a way to get me to the bottom. Taking off my skis and sliding on my rear end was not an option—the slope was too steep and I would just roll, probably crashing into bushes and trees.

That did not sound very fun.

Eventually we came up with a plan.

Well, actually the boys came up with a plan while I was fighting panic.

Jordan uses snow blades, which are very short skis. Their shorter length meant he could maneuver around bushes more easily. So the boys decided he would be my "ride" down the mountain.

We took off my skis, and I held on to a branch, putting my boots on Jordan's shoulders as a brace. His friend held my skis. I am not a light-weight, so my son had to bear my weight as well as the sharp points of my boots as the three of us worked our way down the mountain.

It was a slow process—my grabbing onto one branch at a time, slowly lowering myself, with Jordan below me, keeping my feet on his shoulders.

They did it!

Those boys got me down.

I was so grateful . . . I did a lot of hugging.

They endured that, and Jordan calmly patted me, saying, "We'll see you back at the room, Mom."

Then they took off, as if they hadn't just saved my life!

Together.

Getting through battles requires *together*.

General George S. Patton said it like this:

> Every single man in this Army plays a vital role. Don't ever let up. Don't ever think that your job is unimportant. Every man has a job to do and he must do it. Every man is a vital link in the great chain.[2]

Some people can sing. I mean really sing. Sing so that it touches heaven and changes hearts.

Some can dance with such style and rhythm that it is mind-boggling.

Some can take a swatch of fabric and toss it on the floor, move one piece of furniture and suddenly make a room look amazing.

Some people can take photos that make you feel as if you were there.

Some can paint . . . a room or a canvas or flowers on their nails.

Some can design clothes. Or just create a great outfit by adding a belt, scarf, necklace—whatever! I just know I wouldn't have even thought of it!

Some can make the computer do miraculous things.

Some can smile and welcome us into church or a department store— and they keep smiling even if we have a grumpy face.

Some can organize your closet and your life.

Some are great counselors and give excellent advice.

Some can whisper to dogs or horses.

Some can jump high and run fast.

Some can cook. Really cook. They don't even use a cookbook and it tastes amazing. (These people are *really* good to have on our team!)

Some people can nurse us back to health.

Some can turn a room of fifth-grade boys into well-behaved young men.

And the list goes on and on and on . . .

In the first months after the cancer diagnosis, I realized there was much I would need to change about my life in order to finish strong. I changed my diet, the cleaning products I used, my exercise and rest patterns. So, yeah, there were things that I had done wrong and needed to change. But there were also a few things I had done right to position myself for battle. First, for over 20 years, I had planted myself in the house of God. The psalmist tells us that those who are planted in the house of God will flourish.[3]

Not those who just show up occasionally.

Not those who attend.

Not those who transplant themselves regularly.

But those who are planted.

Whose roots go down deep.

Who are serving and giving.

Who are contributing.

Our lives are designed to flourish when we are planted in the local church, the house of God. Because of that, it is always sad to me when people treat the church so casually. The Bible does not say that our lives flourish when we find the perfect job or spouse. No. Being planted in the house of God brings about a flourishing life (which might well include the perfect job and the perfect spouse).

Some Christians have said, "Well, I am just a part of the universal Church."

Yes, you are.

But I suggest you find a local branch to connect to.

You don't hear soldiers saying that they are a part of the global armed services.

Nope.

They have chosen a branch. They are either in the Army, Navy, Air Force, Marines or Coast Guard.

If someone told you they are a part of the National Basketball Association (NBA), you would probably ask which team. You want to know if they play for the Lakers, the Knicks, the Celtics or the Kings. If they responded that no, they weren't a part of a specific team, they were just in the NBA, you would think they were a little confused.

Same with church. Find one and plant yourself there.

In my years of pastoring and leading in church, I have seen people in battles run from church rather than to it—which makes me sad. The house of God should be the first place we go to when we are hurting.

We are to "dwell" in the house of God, as the psalmist says. What does dwell mean? Well, it means that we "do life" in the house of God. We don't just show up for mealtimes and then run out the door. Yes, we're all home when dinner is on the table, but our being together at home is about so much more than mealtime. We all have chores to do that make home a great place to be. (And some of the time we actually remember to do them!) We spend time together. We talk. Philip and I help with homework. We hug, laugh, cry, sing. We get refreshed so that we can go out and face another day. All of this happens in our home—I think it should happen in the house of God too. Don't just make church a place where you spend an hour on Sunday. Make it a place where you dwell. It should be a place where real people with real lives and real problems can find real help as they worship a real God.

The house of God should be the most creative, energetic, loving, awesome place on the earth. Yes, it is full of imperfect people on a journey, but it is the vehicle God uses to establish His kingdom of love on the earth. The "church of the living God [is] the pillar and foundation of the truth."[4]

Maybe you have encountered judgment and criticism in the house of God, rather than unconditional love.

I am sorry.

At one point in our church, we had a banner that said, "Welcome Home," because we honestly want it to be a place where the lost, confused and hurting come to get help. Home should be a place where you relax, find refreshment, enjoy each other and get battle training.

Another way that I positioned myself well for battle was that I married a warrior, not a wimp. During the first days of our dealing with a frightening diagnosis, Philip was a huge strength. He certainly held me. He even crawled into bed and cried with me. But he also spoke the truth of God's Word over my life. He put Bible verses all over our house. He emailed friends to ask for prayer. When I was afraid, he was courageous. Yes, I made a wise decision when I said "I do" to him over 22 years ago.

And maybe you are looking at your husband and you wonder about his warrior-like abilities. Maybe they are hidden under years of pain.

Keep looking.

Find the warrior in the man you married.

If you are unmarried, then it is definitely essential that you build your family in the house of God. So don't settle. Don't allow your-self to get so desperate that you make a bad choice. Think about the man you are dating—do you see any evidence that he will stand by you and be strong amid the storms of life that will most certainly come your way?

Choose well.

Marry a warrior.

The third way I positioned myself well for battle was that over the years I have built great friendships with fellow warriors. I have lived my life in intimate communion with others. I have not lived an iso-lated life, so when I need to draw on the strengths of other platoon members, they are there.

Now don't get me wrong, building relationships is not always con-venient. Yet I knew that I needed to be creating godly friendships both when it was easy and natural—and when it was difficult and challenging. As a result, when I needed someone to hold up my arms so that an enemy could be defeated, I had so much help.

I had friends fly across oceans to come to doctors' appointments with me.

Across oceans.

Many cooked meals for my family. They drove through the traffic of Los Angeles to deliver them to my home.

Wow.

So many took time out of their busy day to pray for me. I know they all had their own stuff they were dealing with, and yet, they also prayed for me.

Cards and emails covered my wall. And whenever I was discouraged or tired or afraid, I would look at the hundreds of notes—and somehow feel energized.

On one particularly hard day, near the end of treatment, I walked into my office. I had gone to my radiation appointment and then gone to work. I was being just a bit emotional. The doctors were treating my breast with radiation, but somehow the whole process only seemed to be affecting my emotions. Plus, that morning as I stared in my closet, I had a hard time finding anything to wear. I had lost some weight and so my clothes just didn't look that great on me anymore.

Radiation.

Clothes that don't fit.

All this can make a girl emotional!

As I walked into my office, I noticed a package on my desk. There was no return address and no card. I opened the box to find a pair of jeans.

Jeans.

And the miracle is that they fit.

I cried.

Someone had sent me jeans.

A perfect gift in that moment.

Okay, I know that in the big picture of world hunger and the AIDS crisis that this was a *very* small event.

I know that.

But in that moment it was perfect.

And isn't that just like our God?

He gives us just what we need in the moment we need it.

I am and will be forever grateful for the warriors that I have the privilege of being in the platoon with.

Together.

We were meant to do life together.

And doing life together takes work.

Lots of work.

It will take understanding differences.

Because we are different.

The goal is to support each other in our differences. That is what will make the platoon stronger.

Why is it that we get jealous of each other?

Makes no sense.

We are each running in our own lane. Everything I need to fulfill my purpose is in my lane. Every person I am to reach is in my lane. I don't need what is in your lane. You don't need what is in my lane. You and I are to discover our gifts, abilities and talents—many of which are in seed form—and then develop them. As the apostle Paul said, "We each carried our servant assignment. Everything we have and everything we are, are sheer gifts from God. So what is the point of all this comparing and competing? You already have all you need."[5] You and I are on a mission for our King. We each have our own tasks. We can't get distracted by those gifted people running next to us. We should just be glad they are on our team!

Maybe you can sing.

Maybe even an entire song in the right key.

Wish I could.

In fact, sometimes I think that God must have made a mistake. Because I *love* to sing, and I was convinced I would look so cool singing. It's just that no one, besides God, really wants to hear me.

But years ago (before reality set in!), I didn't let that stop me! I thought that I just needed to take voice lessons. I paid good money for months of singing lessons, only to have my voice coach tell me at the end of a session, "Holly, you might want to try the guitar." Not much I could say at that point. I couldn't even pay someone to listen to me!

There are some incredible singers in my platoon. What if I were jealous of them? That jealousy would then cause me to be critical and judgmental and standoffish. My job is *not* to resent the ability or calling of my fellow platoon member—but rather to rejoice in who she is and what she can do.

Our platoon is stronger when each of us is running in our own lane. When each of us is growing in our own gifts and abilities.

How about if we cheer our follow runners on?

Let's encourage each other as we are running.

Not try to trip each other.

Friendly fire kills.

And we need all of us finishing strong.

We also have different personalities. Companies around the world have spent thousands developing profiles for their employees so that they can place each employee in the right spot and so that they all learn to accept each other's differences.

Some of us are the party-in-a-bottle kind of people who can talk to anyone at anytime. These people are energetic, happy and definitely keep things exciting. These folks do have some weaknesses, however. They might be great project starters, just not always great finishers.

Some of us are the ducks-in-a-row kind of people. These people like organization. Their desks are practically works of art—everything is in its proper place. (White Out and spell check were invented by these people!) They are the deep thinkers of the group. They also have weaknesses. While they like perfection, life rarely is, so they have a tendency to become depressed. And that can lead to isolation.

And then some people are the goal-driven ones. They have 10-year goals, 5-year goals, 6-month goals and 5-minute goals! They get a lot done and help the rest of us stay focused. They have a tendency, however, to step on innocent bystanders on the way to reaching their goal. Ouch.

And then there are the people who are the don't-rock-the-boat types. They are easy going and peaceful. They make great counselors because they don't mind listening to your story for the sixth time! These are the ones who, when you ask them what they want to do, they say, "Whatever you want . . . whatever." So, on the down side of things, they have a hard time making a decision—and that just might drive the rest of us nuts!

So, why did I bring all that up?

Well, you do have a personality.

A God-given one.

So does the person next to you.

Yes, we are all on the journey to look like Jesus, but I will do it with my personality and in my skin.

Not yours.

I am sure the weaknesses, and perhaps even the strengths, in me might frustrate you. And because I am a follower of Christ, I am not going to just settle into my weaknesses.

No.

I am working on them.

But the journey might be messy.

Perhaps we come from different cultures.

Our ethnicity might be different.

Our skin might not be the same color.

Our hair might be different textures.

Our words might not sound the same.

I love the fact that in my platoon so many languages are spoken. Definitely comes in handy! I love the accents. Yes, it might make it harder to understand what is said, but the work is worth it. And I love the different colloquial expressions—talk about a rich diversity. My favorite Australian one is: "She spit the dummy." It really is a great one. If you don't know what it means, you will have to go make an Australian friend (Aussies are so much fun to have in your platoon!).

Maybe your family has bazillions of dollars. Or maybe you come from a family on welfare.

Why is it that we let little things like personality differences, cultural differences or economic differences cause separation in our camp?

Most of the people we begin to build friendships with are very different from us.

They have different backgrounds, personalities, baggage, abilities, ways they handle pressure, parenting skills . . . lots of differences that could separate if we don't understand that we are to remain with our platoon.

I once built a friendship with a woman who had been raised with six brothers and so she didn't really know how to do the "girlfriend hang out" thing. She did not understand that clothes were meant for sharing, so I had to be patient while waiting for the new additions to my wardrobe!

And another friend was an only child, so she wasn't very comfortable being open, because she had never done it. She was just very reserved.

And another woman, who is a great friend today, was raised by a family who did not really trust white people—and she herself had been betrayed by a blonde cheerleader type. Enter me into her world! I had to be patient and persistent, not letting her hold on to her prejudice but giving her time to come around.

Sometimes our friends are just in different seasons of life.

Maybe your friend is single. She might have a lot more time to play.

But what if she is now married with three young children—or running a company? She may not be able to spend as much time with you as before. Can you adjust?

What if your friend is in a rough season? Dealing with a few battles of her own?

What if she was fired from her job?

Or maybe she has been trying to get pregnant and, after three intensive procedures, has another miscarriage?

Can you remain the loyal friend during those times?

The truth is that we don't want to see our friends suffer, obviously.

But in the midst of their hard time, we don't want to be like Job's friends, who tried to tell him it was his fault—or his kid's fault. They were quite patronizing and full of hot air, acting like they were the experts. (And there's nothing more annoying than friends who think they are experts in everything!)

This last year, during my battle with cancer, some people said to me . . .

"I believe you are healed; the Bible says it. So I am not going to ask how you are doing anymore, because you are healed!" Well, yeah, I understand what they mean. But such comments are just not very friendly.

As a real friend, you can't minimize your friends' pain.

"Oh, so you lost your job. Well, God will bring you a better one!" That might be true, but a real friend shows that she understands the pain.

"Oh, your friend lied about you. Well, you are better off without him." Again, might be true—it just doesn't help with the immediate pain.

"Oh, you got diagnosed with cancer. Well, there have been so many advances in medical technology that you'll be fine!" Probably true. But what I want to hear is, "I am so sorry you are going through this. I know this might be a scary time. And can I bring chocolate (organic of course!) and come cry with you?"

A real friend does her best to understand, listen and help you look for God in the middle of the battle that might be raging.

And just a confession.

There were some people last year whom I did not want to partner with.

I didn't want to be in their platoon.

In fact, I was mad that I was even meeting them.

I didn't want cancer.

I certainly did not want to be getting radiation treatments every day.

And I did not want to know those people in the radiation waiting room—because I was mad that I was even there in that radiation center in my disgusting robe.

I walked into the room and looked at the floor. I just wanted to be out of there.

After about the fourth day of treatment, I felt a whisper from heaven.

"Holly, look around you."

"No."

But I did.

I saw some very scared, hurting people. People who were in far worse shape than I was.

My heart was touched.

For this season, they became a new circle of friends.

When it came time for my next appointment, I walked in with a smile and asked how everyone was doing. I shared cookies (healthy ones!); I prayed for them. I gave them books. While I was there, I just decided to *be* there.

To connect with the people that God had brought across my path.

Not saying it was easy.

Just did it.

With a very definite purpose, God brings people into our life who are different from us.

Different strengths.

Different backgrounds.

Different personalities.

Different abilities.

We get in trouble when we say we don't need each other. In Paul's letter to the Corinthians, he had a chat with them about this very issue. I guess jealousy and the need to be better than others has been around a long time. In his letter, he challenged them to see themselves as a part of something bigger. He put it this way:

> I want you to think about how all this makes you more significant, not less. A body isn't just a single part blown up into something huge. It's all the different-but-similar parts arranged and functioning together. If Foot said, "I'm not elegant like Hand, embellished with rings; I guess I don't belong to this body," would that make it so? If Ear said, "I'm

not beautiful like Eye, limpid and expressive; I don't deserve a place on the head," would you want to remove it from the body? If the body was all eye, how could it hear? If all ear, how could it smell? As it is, we see that God has carefully placed each part of the body right where he wanted it.

But I also want you to think about how this keeps your significance from getting blown up into self-importance. <u>For no matter how significant you are, it is only because of what you are a part of.</u> An enormous eye or a gigantic hand wouldn't be a body, but a monster. What we have is one body with many parts, each its proper size and in its proper place. No part is important on its own. Can you imagine Eye telling Hand, "Get lost; I don't need you"? Or, Head telling Foot, "You're fired; your job has been phased out"? As a matter of fact, in practice it works the other way—the "lower" the part, the more basic, and therefore necessary. You can live without an eye, for instance, but not without a stomach. When it's a part of your own body you are concerned with, it makes no difference whether the part is visible or clothed, higher or lower. You give it dignity and honor just as it is, without comparisons. If anything, you have more concern for the lower parts than the higher. If you had to choose, wouldn't you prefer good digestion to full-bodied hair?[6]

So what does this mean?

Maybe we could live without those people who are visible—the loud, out-front ones.

Wait.

I'm one of those.

No, I don't think that is what he is saying.

I think maybe it is that as a loud, out-front person, I am really nothing unless I am connected to the unseen—the quiet, the peaceful.

You and I are each significant.

But only because we are a part of something bigger.

The parts are never greater than the sum.

Because we are all a little bit weird, because we all have imperfections, we will all need forgiveness. And to receive it, we must give it.

Do you know the story of Jacob and Esau?

They were twins. Sons of Isaac.

Jacob, the second-born twin, deceived Esau and took the rights of the firstborn from him.

Then Jacob ran for his life.

The two basically lived separate lives, apart from each other for a number of years.

One day, Jacob, who had been the deceiver, knew it was time to go home. He packed up his large family and all of his new wealth and headed home.

He was nervous. He was afraid. He had treated his brother unfairly and now was worried that his brother would kill him. He sent a messenger ahead and said, "Tell my master Esau this: I am coming home with lots of animals and servants, with wealth, and I am hoping for your approval. Love, your servant, Jacob."

Then Jacob prepared a present—goats and rams, camels and cows, bulls and donkeys (when you are trying to get my forgiveness, I really don't need the cows or camels—you can just ask!).

He split up the herds and put space in between them, hoping his brother would be softened by the procession of gifts.

He was hoping that Esau would be glad to see him. Or if not, at least wouldn't kill him.

The night before he was to approach his brother's house, Jacob had a wrestling match with God. When Jacob woke up, he saw Esau and 400 men coming toward him. He stood up and then bowed before his brother seven times, honoring him. He was just a little nervous.

But Esau ran up and embraced him . . . kissed him. And they both wept.

Then Jacob said upon encountering such forgiveness, "When I saw your face, it was as the face of God smiling on me."[7]

Pretty amazing.

When Jacob saw forgiveness, he felt like he was seeing God's face.

Let's be quick to forgive.

Let's give someone else the gift of seeing God's face.

The face of forgiveness.

Again, not saying it will be easy.

Just essential if we are going to fulfill our role as fellow warriors.

We will not win the battle alone.

We have been surrounded with a platoon of fellow warriors whose strengths will help bring victory.

And we need your strength to help lift the sword when a fellow warrior is weary.

Our platoon is not complete without you.

Yeah, we are all a little bit weird, but we do need each other.

Together.

We.

Us.

United we stand.

Divided we fall.

Together.

chapter 7

get dressed!

It was an ordinary Tuesday.

Men kissed their wives good-bye before work.

Kids were getting ready for school.

Women were walking down the street.

Families boarded airplanes.

The hustle and bustle of life in New York City was in full throttle. To most, it seemed like a regular day . . . but this day was anything but ordinary.

A citywide gasp was heard as the first plane crashed into the World Trade Center.

Fear gripped a nation.

Tears wrecked faces.

Screams stung the atmosphere.

And then the second plane hit.

People leaped from the windows to their death.

The towers crumbled and dust clothed the city.

Not one survivor was left on the planes.

The city was in utter chaos and a world was watching.

Was this the end?

Fathers, sons, brothers, husbands, mothers, daughters, friends, lovers, babies would meet eternity that day.

Who would rise to help?

Men and women at every station began to dress themselves for battle. Fireproof pants were pulled on.

Jackets buttoned.

Boots fastened.

Helmets worn.

Axes in tow.

Shields ready.

They would rise.

Everything they had been trained for was now.

They didn't have time to think—they had to do.

Three hundred and forty-three of these heroes breathed their last breath that day.

But they did not quit.

They would not give up.

The New York City Fire Department rose.

They had the armor for this battle.

A city . . . a nation is grateful.

Sometimes we get the romantic picture of what life is like, rather than the reality picture. Over and over again I see young girls in my world make this crucial mistake. Can I save you some heartbreak now?

Stop it.

Don't romanticize everything you see. You will be fighting some battles.

I heard a pastor once say that we are on a battleship, not a cruise ship. Both are vessels that float on water. But their purposes are very different.

Sometimes we dress ourselves in sundresses and sandals (spiritually speaking!) when we should be in camouflage and boots. When we are in the middle of a battle, it is not the time to abdicate our responsibilities, party with our girlfriends or ignore our reality.

It is the time to get our gear on and prepare for battle.

I wonder sometimes if Esther might have gotten a little comfortable in the palace with her king.

Her uncle Mordecai had to appeal to her for the people, saying, "Do not think that because you are in the king's house you alone of all the Jews will escape. For if you remain silent at this time, relief and deliverance for the Jews will arise from another place, but you and your father's family will perish. And who knows but that you have come to royal position for such a time as this?"[1]

Maybe she was having a cruise-ship moment, and it took his reminder to bring her mind and energy back to the battleship—and *sans* sundress, an entire nation was saved.

God would never send us into battle without our armor on. It is armor that we should be very familiar with.

Remember the scene in the movie *Gladiator*, when Russell Crowe's character was putting on his armor?

He did not wonder what it was.

He did not struggle to figure out where the many pieces went.

He was familiar with his armor.

Putting it on was second nature to him.

So it should be with us.

Paul writes to us in Ephesians about the armor of God. He writes from a jail in Rome, where he probably met quite a few Roman soldiers. Their armor from top to bottom was a helmet, a breastplate that was held on by a belt, shoes that were lethal weapons, a shield and, finally, a sword.

Paul urges us to put on the full armor of God so that we can stand against the enemy's schemes.

Battleship.

Not cruise ship.

We must learn to dress ourselves.

God gave us the helmet of salvation.

Today I watched my daughter Paris ride her horse, Elvis.

Quite a name for a thoroughbred. His show name is Slew Suede Shoes. The Slew part of the name comes from his grandsire, Seattle Slew, and you can probably figure out the suede shoes part. Both she and my husband came up with the show name and they are very proud!

Today was a windy day, and Elvis was feeling a bit frisky. For no apparent reason, he started bucking. Paris held on through the first buck, but the second one sent her flying (a mother's worst nightmare!). She landed on her hip and then her head hit the ground hard. I imagine she saw a few stars. The horse ran for the open gate and then galloped down the road to his stall. I ran toward Paris. She jumped up and started running/limping after Elvis.

Do you know why she was basically unhurt?

She had her helmet on.

That is one of the nonnegotiable rules in our family. Every time Paris is on the back of a horse, she must have a helmet on. It certainly isn't because it makes a great fashion statement, or because she likes how her hair looks after taking the helmet off! She wears a helmet because it just might save her life.

And the helmet of salvation will save yours.

The Roman soldiers wore iron helmets that protected their entire head. The helmet consisted of two hinged sidepieces that protected the soldier's jaw and cheekbone; a long piece of metal at the back of the helmet protected the neck. The soldiers knew that one blow to the head could kill, so they did not forget to put on their helmets before going into battle.

You and I are to put on the helmet of salvation. This helmet is designed to guard our minds. In the midst of battle, our mind must be protected. Most battles truly begin and end in the mind. The mind is the source for every action we take, every decision we make and every thought that we allow to linger. Every behavior we exhibit begins in our mind.

The helmet of salvation guards our mind and gives us confidence in Christ. You and I have been saved by what Christ did for us on the cross. God didn't establish a relationship with us because of our goodness. No, we can only come into the presence of God because of what Jesus did for us. No one can take that away.[2]

Before you were in your mother's womb, God called you, set you apart.

He is your source of strength, hope and confidence.

You have to know that you know that you are God's. You belong to Him.

He is your Savior, your Creator, your King . . . your Friend.

You are the loved-beyond-measure daughter of the King.

You are royalty.

The helmet reminds us of all these things.

Make sure yours is on.

The next thing we are to put on is the breastplate of righteousness.

Got any of those in your closet?

The breastplate of the Roman soldier protected the tender part of his body much like the bulletproof vest that our police officers wear today does. The breastplate protects vital organs, including our heart. If we are going to win any battle, our spiritual heart has to be protected. Our heart must be right with God.

When we walk in the righteousness of God, it is a weapon of defense against all lies, plans and accusations of our enemy, the devil. Being right with God means knowing who we are . . . His beloved daughter. Jesus put us in right standing with the Father. When we know that, we can defeat the lies of the enemy.[3]

The breastplate also enables us to carry ourselves with honor, to walk uprightly, to boldly take on anything that comes our way. As warriors, we are to be people with honor and integrity—doing what's right, even if it is not always what we might feel like doing.

Hitting the gym even if you are a little tired.

Engaging your mind instead of zoning out in front of the TV.

Declaring the tips you earned on your taxes, even if your friends don't.

Pursuing a relationship with a new friend, even if you are shy.

Showing up on time for your job, even if your boss isn't there.

Helping your husband find his keys (for the hundredth time!).

Eating a salad instead of that double cheeseburger.

Forgiving when you would rather not.

Telling the truth, when a lie seems easier.

Making time to spend with God, even though there seems to be no time.

You get the picture.

Walking in the righteousness of God helps us keep our honor and integrity while allowing room for honest mistakes. It also guards our heart, from which our life flows.[4]

What is flowing out of you? We must put on our breastplate of righteousness.

Next, we are to gird our waist with the belt of truth.

I don't really wear a belt to hold up my pants, although I am aware some people do. I have a few belts, but they really serve no purpose other than to make a fashion statement. However, for the Roman soldier, the belt was a very important part of the uniform. It held the weapons that the soldier would need. He would put the belt on first and tie it firmly in place. It was tied so tightly that no matter how tough the battle was or how much the soldier moved, it stayed in place. The belt had to be in the right place in order for the soldier to have easy access to his weapons.[5]

Truth holds things in place for us. Our ability to use our weapons, and even our protection, comes from having God's truth as our belt.

His truth must be our foundation if we are going to wage war
against the enemy.[6]

And how do we know the truth?

We hear it. We all have to find a church that is alive, a place that
will speak life over us. We should be investing in some teaching CDs
that can help us on our journey. (It also might keep us from sinning
when that person cuts us off on the freeway!)

We read it. He will speak to us through it. It is our manual for living. How about also reading some books that inspire and give
practical insight into the Word?

We understand it. We need only ask God to show us. The Holy Spirit
will bring wisdom to us. We need to make some friends who also
desire truth. If we're having difficulty, then we should find an older
woman in the church who will answer our questions, and who
doesn't think we're crazy when we ask them.

Now come the shoes.

The really good part!

"And with your feet fitted with the readiness that comes from the
gospel of peace."[7]

What is peace? The freedom of the mind from annoyance, distraction, anxiety or an obsession.

Imagine that you can get to a place in your mind that is free from
annoyance (in spite of toddlers and teenagers); distraction (from
Mr. Universe or the good-looking guy at the gym!); anxiety
(because your hot-water heater just blew up and the mortgage is
due); and obsession (over that voice that constantly tells you what
you're not).

There is a sure-footed stability in Christ that we must step into.

The shoes that the Roman soldiers wore looked more like vicious golf shoes than our modern-day combat boots. Conical hobnails or spikes were placed on the soles of the soldier's thick sandals, which provided him with leverage for a strong stance. These shoes also provided the soldier with balance for easier walking over rough ground. Those spikes definitely came in handy for walking all over the enemy. Yikes![8]

The peace of Christ gives us that same strong stance. It offers us the balance we need to walk over rough ground . . . a bad spot in marriage, a friendship on the rocks, a betrayal in the family.

The shoes of the Roman soldier kept him stable.

Good idea.

Warriors are stable.

They are not led by every passing emotion. Emotions can be extremely powerful, but every emotion has to yield to the submission of Christ.

Just because we *feel* something does not mean we must act on it. Getting sentimental about a person or situation can knock you off course. But a warrior is stable enough to be at peace in the storm—a warrior chick is not swayed by the emotion of the moment.

However, if our mind is cluttered with doubt, disillusionment, distraction, disappointment—all those big *D* words—we will lack the ability to see the opportunities that are right in front of our face.

So, remember, put on the shoes of peace.

Let His peace guide your every step.

Now that our conical hobnailed sandals are on (!), we must pick up the shield of faith.

Roman soldiers used a large oblong shield that protected them from arrow attacks. It was made of wood and was covered with leather or metal. During times of combat, the enemy would launch a barrage of arrows toward the soldiers.

The arrows often were wrapped in cloth, soaked in pitch and then set on fire. These flaming arrows could inflict serious damage. However, the leather covering on the Roman soldier's shield was often soaked in water so that when the fiery arrow hit the shield, it was extinguished.

You and I have an enemy—Satan—and he continues to shoot his fiery arrows at us. I don't know what missiles he has fired your way—maybe fear, doubt, guilt, shame, sickness, discouragement or hopelessness. But I do know that the only way you can extinguish those arrows is with your shield of faith.

Where are you placing your faith? Do you believe that no matter how fierce the battle, your heavenly Father is watching over you? Is your faith in Him and His promises?[9]

Every year, I meet new women on a journey toward healing. Some have been sexually abused; some are struggling with depression; some have been orphaned through the loss of a parent; the list goes on. And that is the nature of life. King Solomon tells us that time and chance happen to us all.[10]

But you know who makes it to the promised land of healing? Those who put their faith in God.

Not a method, not a person, not anything else.

The ones who rise over and over and refuse to accept anything less than what God has for them. Solomon also tells us that though a righteous woman falls seven times, she rises again.[11]

Well, since you already pulled out that breastplate of righteousness from your dresser drawer, then you are a righteous woman. So, even when (notice I did not say "if") you really mess up and fall on your face, rise.

And when someone else knocks you on your butt, rise.

And when the grind of daily life puts you on your back, rise.

The just shall live by faith.[12]

We rise by faith.

Sometimes that is all we have.

When I faced a death sentence, at first, all I had was faith. It is what helped me rise when I was on my back, with a tear-stained face.

Now, forget the tissue! Pick up that shield, you warrior, and rise.

Finally, you need a weapon.

God gave us a sword.

Very cool.

The sword of the Spirit, which is the Word of God.

While the sword that Roman soldiers used was about 18 inches long and sharp on both sides, the offensive weapon that we have been given is the Word of God. The Greek for "word" in this verse in Ephesians is *rhema*. *Rhema* implies an utterance, a spoken word. In Hebrews, we are told that the Word of God is sharper than any two-edged sword. So let's use it!

When the devil was trying to mess with Jesus in the wilderness, Jesus fought him by speaking the Word of God back to him. Three times the devil tried to tempt Jesus, and three times Jesus rebuked him with Scripture. After the devil's third attempt, Jesus cried, "Away from me, Satan! For it is written: 'Worship the Lord your

God, and serve him only.'"[13] It was the spoken Word that brought victory.

Every warrior needs a battle cry!

She was shocked when she was diagnosed with Hodgkin's disease. She was newly married.

She was in a brand-new city, 3,000 miles from home.

Who was going to help them?

What were they going to do?

They knew they couldn't make it through this battle.

Not by themselves.

They enlisted their friends, their families and their church for this fight.

One day, after a session of chemotherapy, she found herself over her bathroom toilet throwing up.

Her hair was gone.

Her strength was evaporating.

She could barely stand, but she decided to rise.

Something inside of her was greater than her circumstances.

She began to shout her battle cry, "I don't know why this is happening to me, but God, YOU HAVE A PLAN FOR MY LIFE! YOU HAVE GIVEN ME A FUTURE AND A HOPE! YOU SENT YOUR WORD AND HEALED MY DISEASE!" Her words began to clothe her for battle.

She refused to give in to the facts.

Sarah and her husband, Dave, held on to the truth.

Thank you, Sarah.

Warriors have a battle cry. Men are especially good at this. Lots of grunting, shouting and, well, more grunting. What is your battle cry? If it's more Yorkshire terrier than pit bull, then it's time to start grunting!

David had a battle cry and it was Truth.

I bet Goliath looked pretty terrifying.

Hello, he was a giant.

But David also knew His God and he knew this was a battle reserved for Him.

> David answered, "You come at me with sword and spear and battle-ax. <u>I come at you in the name of the God-of-the-Angel Armies</u>, the God of Israel's troops, whom you curse and mock. This very day God is handing you over to me. I'm about to kill you, cut off your head, and serve up your body and the bodies of your Philistine buddies to the crows and coyotes. The whole earth will know that there's an extraordinary God in Israel. And everyone gathered here will learn that God doesn't save by means of sword or spear. <u>The battle belongs to God—he's handing you to us on a platter!</u>"[14]

Woo-hoo!

What a battle cry that was!

I love that "no guts, no glory" attitude!

You might be staring Goliath in the face.

Or the kneecaps.

But you must know that the battle belongs to God.

You must believe that God is who He says He is.

The Great I AM.

And that He will do what He said He would do.

The fight is not with your giant.

It is with your mind.

The fight is to believe the truth.

What is your battle cry?

God will hand over the head of your giant on a silver platter (after all, warrior princesses get the silver ones), if you will believe in His Word.

Speaking of words, did you know that women speak an average of 15,000 to 20,000 words a day . . . whew! So yeah, we speak a lot of words!

I am challenging you to consider what you are saying with your words. The power of life and death is in your tongue. Remember, your words are your sword!

You and I create an environment for good or evil with our words— and guess what? We will have to live in the world we create.

It is tempting to use negative words to describe every situation we encounter.

"My boss did this . . ."

"Can you believe my husband . . ."

"Did you hear what she did to me . . ."

"I'll never be able to . . ."

God asks us to use our words to change negative into positive. Stop talking about your problems (that is actually perpetuating the problem), but open your mouth about solutions.

Jesus tells us to speak *to* the problem.

Don't just think (code for worry) about the problem and pray for it. *Speak* to it!

David spoke to his very big problem (Goliath) by speaking about his very big God. Words will make or break us. Solomon warns us that we can be ensnared by the words of our mouth.[15]

Negative words also put us on the defense.

God intended for you and me to live on the offense, shooting the ball, making the enemy nervous about our scoring—not the other way around! The enemy should not make you nervous! He shouldn't be shooting baskets in your court! You were born for the offense.

So, boldly confess God's word . . . 20,000 words!

Make sure yours (at least most of them) are deliberate, thoughtful, purposeful!

In my battle this year, I have spent hours walking in my room, quoting the Word of God out loud. When the threats of the enemy sound off in my head, I just make my shouts louder! Speak His Word.

And do you know what? You have to practice to engage in this kind of battle. I have read many books about warriors from many different countries and different eras, and the one thing they all did was practice. They spent hours practicing with their swords. They practiced until their swords felt like an extension of their own arm.

Become familiar with God's Word . . . so familiar that in the midst of your unseen battles you can readily speak it out.[16]

Sometimes there is no thinking, only doing. And when you are under pressure, what you really believe about yourself, about life and about God comes out. So, when life seems to be falling apart, what comes out of you? Because what is in us is what will come out of us.

What happens to you when you are squeezed?

Do you immediately throw up your hands and quit?

Do you huff and puff and say, "This stuff always happens to me!"

Do you blame other people?

Do you take it out on the ones you love the most?

Do you hibernate on the couch with the remote control?

Do you wear the trial all over you?

How about if we speak the truth to our situation? The Word has got to become second nature to us. It must be our first response to everything if we are to win our battles.

And guess what else (oh no, Holly, not another thing . . .)?

Battles don't just come one at a time.

Wouldn't it be great if they did?!

That would just be so neat and tidy.

But life rarely is.

Haven't you noticed?

You know, your car engine heater blew up . . .

and the mortgage is due . . .

and money is tight . . .

and your kid gets in trouble at school . . .

and the other one flunks out of college . . .

and someone you love ends up in the hospital.

It seems to be everything all at once.

I was diagnosed with cancer and so began waving my sword.

I declared the truth of God's Word over my body. I was fighting for my life.

He is the LORD, who heals me![17]

With long life He will satisfy me and show me His salvation![18]

And then in the middle of the fight for my health, someone—actually lots of someones—told me of friends and loved ones who had been cancer-free for a while and then died.

Aaaghh!!

I have no idea why people felt the need to do that.

So there I was, fighting for my life, and fear tried to get a foothold. I had to swing my sword in another direction, while keeping it swinging in the first direction.

I had to fight fear.

I had to say out loud—very loudly:

The LORD is with me; I will not be afraid![19]

I will not be afraid of the terror of the night because I dwell in the secret place of the Most High. A thousand may fall at my side, ten thousand at my right hand, but it will not come near me![20]

And *then* in the middle of double-sword swinging, I had to deal with a lawsuit—a ridiculous one that the enemy was using to distract me. Basically the message that God had put in my mouth was being attacked.

And I admit at first I was surprised by the hatefulness of it all.

So in the middle of radiation treatments, I had to go before attorneys and listen to the horrible things that were being said about me. In the car heading home, I cried, and then I pulled out my sword.

Weapons made to attack me won't be successful![21]

I am the head and not the tail![22]

Now as I was triple-sword swiping, some financial issues came up, because many of my medical treatments were not covered by insurance. Philip and I had planned a trip to celebrate 20 years of marriage and the fact that I was still breathing. And I did not want to give it up! So of course, the enemy went for our finances (he is so predictable). But I pointed the sword that direction too!

Because I tithe, the windows of heaven are open over my life, pouring out blessing.[23]

God will supply all my needs according to His riches in glory.[24]

Jesus came so that I might have an abundant life . . . so thief, you cannot steal from me![25]

And then because a warrior is never in battle alone, I had to do a little sword waving on behalf of some fellow warriors who were in battles. One was in the middle of a marriage crisis (we've all been there!), so I pulled out my sword on her behalf.

Marriage is honorable among all.[26]

He is rejoicing with her, the wife of his youth![27]

Okay, so all this sword waving was starting to get exhausting—and there were moments when I was overwhelmed.

Maybe you have been there, too.

Maybe you are there right now, doing a lot of sword waving, feeling a little weak, asking God to take away the pain.

Well, there is good news:

Each time he said, "My grace is all you need. My power works best in weakness." So now I am glad to boast about my weaknesses, so that the power of Christ can work through me. That's why I take pleasure in my weaknesses, and in the insults, hardships, persecutions, and troubles that I suffer for Christ. For when I am weak, then I am strong.[28]

I am stronger today. And it is because I got to the end of my strength. It was His strength that helped me swing my sword.

And just so you know, in the middle of all this battling, I wrote a book—just to stick it to the enemy. What he meant for evil, God meant for good. So like any mature warrior princess would, I stuck my tongue out and went "na na, na na" to the enemy ☺.

Paul sends the Ephesians off to battle with a challenge: "This is no afternoon athletic contest."[29] He is reminding us again that this is a battleship (remember, wear the breastplate, not the sundress).

In painting a picture of the modern-day warrior, I have tried to make the weapons Paul refers to in Ephesians relevant to you and me. But I also think there are some more modern-day weapons at our disposal.

Because what we fight for helps to define who we are.

Every battle might need different weapons.

The modern-day warrior might be armed with a hug if a loving touch is needed.

She might be armed with a cool cloth to wipe a sick person's forehead if that is what is needed.

She might be armed with a hammer if building a home for the homeless is needed.

She might be armed with an adoption certificate if rescuing a child is what is needed.

She might be armed with hope if giving hope is needed.

She might be armed with money if giving money is needed.

We have to be dressed for battle.

Whatever that battle might be.

So don't forget your checklist:

☐ Helmet of salvation

☐ Breastplate of righteousness

☐ Belt of truth

☐ Shoes of peace

☐ Shield of faith

☐ Sword of the Spirit

Now never leave home without them!

chapter 8

who's the boss?

The heaviness of responsibility was setting in with the sunset.

He was troubled.

Sorrowful to the point of death.

"Stay here and keep watch with me," He urged them.

Agony swept through the lines on His face.

The lump in His throat was rising.

He made it a little farther and fell to His knees.

Was there another way?

Face to the ground, He begged, "Father, if it is possible, may this cup be taken from me. Yet not as I will, but as You will."

He turned in the garden to draw strength from His brothers, His friends.

He found them sleeping . . . did they not know?

Could they not discern the time?

Did they not know the season?

"Could you not even keep watch with me one hour?" He asked Peter. "Watch and pray so that you may not fall into temptation," He urged him again.

Again He walked away to talk to His God.

Face to the ground, sweating blood, He prayed again, "My Father, if it is not possible for this cup to be taken away unless I drink it, may Your will be done."

He heard noise on the horizon.

Voices of soldiers, chains rattling, torches blazing.

It was time.

Settled, He rose with confidence.

Though He knew the road ahead, He also knew He could trust the authority to which He had yielded.

Though He understood who His enemy was, He understood the authority He had been given.

"Who is it that you want?" He asked the mob.

"Jesus of Nazareth."

"I am He."

His hour had come and He yielded all of Himself to the cause.

To you . . . me . . . us.

We owe our eternity to this single act of surrender.

Warriors understand authority.

A policeman has the authority to pull us over if we are speeding or if we don't stop at the stop sign, but he has to choose to exercise that authority.

He has the authority to give us tickets if we stay in the white zone at the airport (you know . . . the loading and unloading only zone). In November 2001, Philip was dropping me off at the airport and we were right in the middle of a big hug and kiss good-bye when the airport policeman yells out, "No kissing! [He actually *did* say 'no kissing.'] Move your car along!" I guess he was choosing to exercise his authority. I did not see much wrong with a kiss, nor did I think I was very terrorist looking, but maybe our car was blocking his view of something else. I don't know. I just know that we shortened our embrace, and Philip pulled away from the white curb!

A policeman *can* just watch us speed by, roll through that stop sign or stay parked in the white zone.

He has authority.

He just has to use it.

So do we.

We have not been sent to earth as warriors without authority.

Because I belong to Jesus, I have been given authority.

But I have to choose to exercise the authority that has been given to me.

I can use it to fight my fight as the warrior I have been called to be.

Or I can lie down and be defeated.

My choice.

So what authority has been given to us?

We have been given the authority to make choices.[1]

Heaven and earth are witnesses to our choices.

We were not created as puppets.

We have a free will.

So we can make choices.

Good ones.

Bad ones.

Either.

This means that we can't blame God for the consequences of our decisions—because we have been given the authority to make them.

If we choose to eat a diet of fried everything and very little green stuff, then we will become unwell. And we cannot blame our Commander. He has given us the authority to choose well.

If we choose to not train or discipline our children, then we cannot blame God when they are out of control. We have been given the authority to make the choices surrounding how we raise our kids.

Not to choose is also a choice.

Probably not the strongest.

The goal is to make the strongest and wisest choice in this moment.

Choices that propel our life forward.

Choices that produce the future we want.

Choices that positively impact those around us.

Choose well.

The great thing is that we are not on our own. Jesus said that as we step out, He steps out with us. He is with us forever—to the very end of the age.

We have been given the authority to forgive.[2]

It was a big bother to the Pharisees when Jesus operated in forgiveness. Because when He forgave, miracles happened. They challenged whether He truly could forgive sins.

You might get challenged too.

By your emotions.

Because, honestly, none of us ever feels like forgiving.

When someone hurts me, my first thought is, *I hope lightning strikes her house . . . her yard . . . or at least her shoe collection!*

Yep.

Forgiveness is never my first thought.

Sorry to have to admit that.

For me, forgiveness usually begins with the second thought.

It always starts in my head.

A decision of my will.

I do it because Jesus said that if I don't forgive, my sins won't be forgiven. And I have plenty of sins that have been and will need to be forgiven.

I know that if I don't exercise forgiveness, there will be consequences. I will be dealing with strife, heaviness and a sense of oppression.

A few years ago someone who had been close to me really hurt my heart. This person just decided to attack. Mainly because the way I do life is different from the way she does hers. Rather than just agreeing that it's okay for us to see things differently, she attacked. She could only see me as wrong, not just different.

So that hurt.

And I wanted to send one of those lightning bolts or at least someone to give her a good smack!

I held onto my hurt for months. I felt justified in feeling hurt. I told the story of betrayal over and over, to anyone who would listen. I wanted everyone to feel my pain. I was stressed and had no peace.

I was not letting go.

And that was the problem. As much as I wanted to be free from this person, I couldn't be. Because my unforgiveness attached us.

So I made a decision to forgive.

I made it daily for a while.

Something interesting happened as I forgave.

I started feeling compassion for this person.

Forgiveness moved from my head to my heart.

Peace began to fill my life.

The stress left.

To this day we are not great friends, but I can be kind to this person. And I am so glad to be free from the stress. Peace in my soul is a good thing.

In 2006, we were shocked to hear of a mentally disturbed man barging into an Amish schoolhouse and brutally murdering young girls. What a horrible and tragic event in a relatively peaceful community.

The murder made headlines.

What didn't make as many headlines was the Amish community's response to this tragedy.

Within 48 hours, a group of Amish went to the home of the murderer to see his wife and children.

They did not go to yell or blame.

They went to extend forgiveness.

Forgiveness.

They said that, yes, the hurt was massive.

But they don't balance hurt with hate.

They balance it with love and forgiveness.

Wow.

You and I have been given the authority to forgive.

Let's use it.

We have also been given the authority to sow.[3]

A truly amazing gift.

If you don't like your life right now, no worries! You can change it. All you have to do is sow different seeds. Your life right now is the result of seeds you have sown in the past.

It really isn't that complicated.

If we sow apple seeds, we get apple trees.

If we sow apricot seeds, we get apricot trees.

If we sow love, we receive love.

If we sow forgiveness, we receive forgiveness.

If we sow kindness, we receive kindness.

If we give grace, we receive grace.

If we are patient, patience comes back to us.

If we sow money, we receive money.

It would be silly if we thought we could get a peach tree from a grape seed, and yet many of us live our life that way.

In the early years, I was really doing nothing to build my marriage. I was grumbling about how bad it was. The seeds of whining, complaining and being critical started to sprout. My words were producing a harvest and I did not like it. I blamed the harvest for a while.

Nothing happened. Not until I changed the seeds I was sowing.

Maybe as we take an honest look at our life, we might find that we have no great friends. And maybe it is because we have been so focused on what we need in a friend that we have stopped giving. We have been so focused on the kind of friend that we want that we have stopped being that kind of friend. As soon as we stop giving, we stop receiving.

I was watching a show that Oprah Winfrey did in which she gave the people in the audience some money, and then they had the opportunity to give it away. She asked them to give it to someone in need. What they found was that as they gave, more came to them. People they didn't even know joined with them so that what they ultimately gave to the person in need was far greater than the initial amount.

Instead of getting frustrated at the life you might now have, take an honest look at the seeds you have been sowing.

What you sow you will reap. That's how it works.

We also have been given the authority to control our thought life.[4]

We can't always control the first thought that barges through our mind, but we can control the second and the third and the fourth. We must take an honest look at our thoughts. Do they line up with the truth? Or have our imagination and our fears had a field day?

Maybe our friend gave us a funny look.

So now we think, *What's up with her? She looks mad at me. What right does she have to be mad at me? Who does she think she is? She hasn't been that great of a friend anyway!*

Our thoughts have now taken a downward spiral. And the truth could be that she was thinking about her bad day at work or the fact that she hasn't figured out what to serve for dinner tonight or the fact that her shoes are killing her. Her look most likely has nothing to do with us. But because we have failed to control our thoughts, our friendship might be in trouble.

A proverb warns us that we are what we think.[5] Our thoughts control our actions, so we must exercise the authority we have been given and take our thoughts captive. We cannot dwell on what will not produce life. So many things that lead to our destruction begin with a thought.

Fear . . . the fear that paralyzes, begins with a thought.

Hatred . . . the hatred that destroys, begins with a thought.

Anger . . . the anger that damages, begins with a thought.

Apathy . . . the apathy that defeats, begins with a thought.

Paranoia . . . the paranoia that devastates, begins with a thought.

Peace . . . the peace that calms, begins with a thought.

Joy . . . the joy that brings victory, begins with a thought.

Love . . . the love that heals, begins with a thought.

Kindness . . . the kindness that changes lives, begins with a thought.

We have been given the authority to manage our thoughts.

Let's use it.

But our relationship with authority doesn't end here, with our wielding it. We are also under it.

Jesus did only what the Father said.

He was under authority.

Which is why He *had* authority—all the authority under heaven and on Earth.

He had authority over sickness, disease and the demonic realm, because He was under authority.

And yet lots of us balk at authority.

We want it.

We just don't want to be under it.

But to be entrusted with authority, we have to be under authority.

I remember once when I was about to discipline my five-year-old son, he cried out, "You're not the boss of me!" From our earliest years, we resist yielding to authority.

As a parent of young children, we can see what is better for them.

We know that if they eat all of their Halloween candy in one night, they will be sick.

We know that if they run down the stairs with scissors, they could get hurt.

We know that if they stay up too late, they will not do well in school tomorrow.

We know that no matter what our 13-year-old promises, no matter how many times he asks, we are not going to give him the keys to the car.

They are not ready for that part of the journey yet. Are we just mean, controlling people who don't want our children to have fun?

No.

We love them and want the best for them.

How do we know what might be best?

We have been given a certain amount of wisdom to see the big picture.

I just can't imagine a warrior questioning his commander: "I am absolutely not going to be in a platoon with that person."

I wonder if we haven't said words similar to these to God? Don't you think He sees the big picture? And I would imagine He is trying to get all of His warriors in place.

And if He is going to be successful, then we need to follow His orders.

But what does that mean in our life?

In the movie *GI Jane*, the character portrayed by Demi Moore is given leadership over her platoon during one of the last crucial training exercises. Some of the men do not like the fact that a woman is in charge and so do not obey her orders or follow her lead. Their rebellion causes the whole platoon to be captured and two of the members to be tortured. We may not always like our commanders, and yet we are asked to yield to them.

I met Shanelle about 10 years ago while she was attending the University of Southern California. A very intelligent woman, she soon graduated with an engineering degree. After she had been working for a few months at her first job, which she had been thrilled to get, she came to me complaining about her boss. She claimed that she knew more than he did. He was too difficult to work for and didn't listen to her ideas. He never admitted when he was wrong, which was often, nor did he give her credit for good ideas she had come up with. She didn't think she could take it anymore. I agreed with her that it sounded like a difficult situation, and then asked her if she wanted some help in dealing with it. She replied, "Yes." Our conversation then basically went something like this:

"Shanelle, do you believe this is the job that will use your skills effectively?"

"Yes."

"Are there still things you can learn from this company?"

"Yes."

"What do you think your job as an employee is?"

"I guess it is to do the work I am asked to do and do it well."

"Are you doing that?"

"Well, my boss makes it so hard!"

"Yes, it sounds like it, but really, who said life was easy? Your job as his employee is to learn from him, to be a good representative of him, to adapt yourself to his requirements and to be faithful to do good work—that is, if you want a promotion."

She assured me that she did want to advance in the company and that she was willing to make changes in her attitude. It wasn't an easy task, but she began to yield to her boss and be supportive. She quit complaining about him and began to do the work he asked without having an "I know better" attitude (and in many instances she did know better—that was what made it a real challenge!). In a few years, she was promoted to the position of vice president of her company, where she was the highest paid woman executive. At every level along the way, her superiors saw how hard she worked, no matter who her boss was, and so they kept promoting her. She even passed up her initial boss on her way to the top.

Shanelle was promoted time and again over other men and women who didn't understand this concept of following orders. No, she wasn't a doormat. She expressed her opinions whenever they were requested. But she was promoted over men and women who were trying to fight their way to the top because she chose instead to respect her boss's position, whether or not she respected him as an individual. She continued to find favor within the company and with her clients all over the world.

Two years later, and as a direct result of her talent and her understanding this concept so well, she was offered and accepted a position as an officer in the United Nations, where she has had global influence. And now, just a few years later, as a very young woman, she is one the directors of UNICEF. She went from being a frustrated, low-level engineer to become one of the most influential women in an amazing global organization. She now spends her time with presidents and heads of state.

I am so glad she understood the authority issue, because it enabled God to entrust her with authority. And I think He is looking for warriors who get it.

The writer of the book of Hebrews tells us to "obey our leaders and submit to their authority. They keep watch over us as men who must give an account. Obey them so that their work will be a joy, not a burden, for that would be of no advantage to us."[6]

I am sure this is not the most popular Scripture in the Bible. For many years, I wasn't even aware it was in there. But I have learned that if I want the benefits of the authority given to me, then I must yield to authority. And obviously we don't yield to corrupt authority, but we must learn to defer to a higher authority.

As a citizen of the United States, I am submitted to the government of our country and its president. Do I necessarily agree with him and all of the decisions he makes? No, but I must still submit to the *position* of the presidency. I pay taxes and stop at red lights (well . . . most of them!) because I am submitted to the laws in my country.[7] If I want to enjoy the benefits of my country, I must yield to its laws.

Solomon, the wisest man on Earth, said that where there is no vision, no redemptive revelation of God, the people perish; but that she who keeps the law of God, <u>which includes that of man</u>, is blessed happy, fortunate and enviable.[8]

What if David had not yielded to his father's request to take some sandwiches to his brothers on the front line of battle?

What if he had said something like, "I just don't feel like it, Dad. They should have taken their own food. That is a long way to go, and besides, I am not responsible for them!"

What if he had said something like that?

Something that thousands of teenaged boys might have said.

I think that if he had not yielded to his father's request, then he would have missed his moment.

Goliath was his moment.

David wouldn't have gone to the front lines.

He wouldn't have seen the giant taunting the army of God.

He wouldn't have gotten invited into the palace.

I think God orchestrated the whole thing.

God was orchestrating David's promotion.

Just what might be waiting on the other side of your obedience?

Warriors are committed to fighting today's battle.

The psalmist cried out to his God, "Here I am, . . . waiting for directions to get me safely through enemy lines."[9]

Does that sound like any prayer that you've prayed lately?

Generals don't give soldiers a plan for the whole war—just for what they have to do next. God has an excellent long-range plan.[10]

Really.

I think we can trust the Creator of the universe with His creation.

We want the whole plan, but we were actually made to have faith for . . .

THIS DAY.

THIS BATTLE.

I don't imagine that the CEO of IBM gives every detail of his 20-year plan to the first-year programmer. It would probably distract her from her task today. I doubt the film director reveals to the caterer his reason for directing a scene a certain way. It might distract him from today's job, and might even produce undue stress.

Stress and fear come when we take our eyes off now.

We have been created to have faith for this moment.

For now.

In middle of battle, we can't see the whole battlefield.

Just today's fight.

Looking back, I can see that most of the stress I dealt with during my cancer battle came when I worried about what *would* happen.

What if they didn't get all the cancer out with surgery?

Could I really eat this healthy for the rest of my life?

What would seven weeks of radiation do to my body?

What if one of the side effects was a weakened lung?

What if the cancer came back?

What if . . . ?

What if . . . ?

So much of my anxiety came from my worries about "what if."

What ifs are not questions for this moment.

And you and I have been made to have faith in this moment.

Now.

Once I realized that all I had to do was have faith for this moment, then peace came. I did not need to know the answers to all of my what ifs. I just needed the strength to get through the present day's treatment.

All of the heroes of Hebrews chapter 11—Abel, Enoch, Noah, Abraham, Isaac, Jacob, Moses, Joseph, Rahab . . . and the list goes on—had now faith. They did not worry about what might come. They just had faith for the moment they were in.

The fight of faith is a day-to-day fight.

Even Jesus told us not to worry about tomorrow—that each day has enough trouble of its own.[11]

I am not saying that living in the moment, with faith, is easy. But if we are going to live with as little stress as possible, then we must relinquish our need to understand the whole war. Let's just focus on today's battles.

Thank God that His mercy is new every morning.

And thank God that He directs the battle each day.

I just have to listen to His voice. If I am going to successfully navigate any battle, I must be listening for His direction.

> In the first days of Operation Desert Storm in 1991, the primary objective was to take out radar sites and all command-and-control capabilities. The strategy was to blind the enemy and cut off communications between the soldiers and their leaders.[12]

Hard to win a battle if you can't communicate with the one who gives direction—with the one whose eyes can see the bigger plan.

My husband, Philip, is a wonderful leader. And over the years he has had to learn how to lead. He has had to learn how to make his instructions clear so that the church staff can carry out his directions. And at the same time, as a staff, we have had to become adept at listening to his voice and recognizing what he means in any given situation. Peace comes when we are all on the same page.

As a parent, I have had to get very clear in what I am expecting from my children. And they have gotten better at understanding my voice.

As the director of GodChicks, I have learned to give clearer directions, and as a result, my team has been enabled to better follow my leadership. There are many times when they just know that I would or wouldn't like something. Why? Because they have gotten good at listening to the direction I give.

As a Christian, I am getting better at listening to the direction given by my heavenly Father.

He is clear in what He wants.

His Word paints a comprehensible picture of what He requires.

Last year I spent two weeks in a hospital, and I was alone for about five of those days. One morning, I woke up very early—even before the sun!—and I heard the voice of my Commander from deep within. The night before had been a stressful one as I lay worrying about what all the tomorrows would bring, and in the morning I heard His voice asking me to trust Him. Reassuring me that He would be with me all day throughout all of the treatments.

A simple thing really.

But the peace that came with His voice was indescribable.

Hearing His voice brings not just peace but also wisdom. We cannot lead unless we listen.

Leadership comes with responsibility.

> Every person should see herself as a leader called by God. And we have each been given a sphere of influence that God expects us to take care of.[13]

During the Iraq war, there were some CBS News reporters embedded with a U.S. battalion. One of the reporters was Byron Pitts, and he was impressed with the leadership of a captain, recalling what happened one particular day.

There was one point where one of the young corporals said, "Sir, we spotted where the fire is coming from. There are three people, let me take the shot."

The captain said, "Have you identified their weapons?"

The corporal admitted, "No, sir."

The captain reaffirmed, "Don't take the shot until you can confirm the weapon."

Even though the corporal kept pushing, the captain wouldn't allow anyone to return fire. Moments passed and they saw three heads bobbing up and down. The Marines all assumed that these three were the enemy. Within moments, however, a man, his wife, and daughter stood up. Because this captain made the right call, three people are alive today.

We talked later about it. I said, "How were you so calm?"

He said, "Byron, trust me, on the inside I was as frightened as anyone. But I had to keep my men calm. And they looked to me for direction."[14]

The young captain made a very wise decision, yet it could have turned out badly for him. War is a dangerous enterprise. In several other situations, the sad deaths of American troops have resulted from their well-intentioned efforts to help Iraqi children. Good intentions do not always make up for bad decisions.[15] But the captain in this story did understand a very important part of leadership—those under a leader look to her for guidance on how to handle a situation.

As I have mentioned, I was very aware as I entered the battle with cancer that I would have thousands of eyes watching to see how I handled the challenge. Why were they watching? They saw me as an example, someone to follow. However I faced my battle is how they would handle theirs.

Would I freak out?

Would I lose it?

I felt a great sense of obligation to remain faith filled. And actually the only way I could do that was to look to my Commander.

Once we have listened to our Commander, our task today becomes *our* responsibility. Which means success or failure rests with us.

Warriors don't blame.

We don't point a finger at someone else.

Even if we might have been a victim of someone else's cruelty, we accept the responsibility to change and overcome.

Recently, I heard on the news about some American evacuees who had left Lebanon. They were doing a lot of whining about the lousy way they had been evacuated. I thought they should have been grateful they had escaped to safety. Since 2004 the State Department had been warning those traveling to Lebanon that they were taking a risk in being there. So these people who had disregarded the advice of those in charge were now complaining about their "inefficient" rescue. None of them took responsibility for having brought their families to Lebanon in the first place. Not very warrior-like behavior.

Warriors do not whine!

I love the story of the Roman soldier who came to Jesus, telling Him about his servant who was ill. Jesus offered to go to the sick man and heal him. The soldier's response amazed Jesus.

> The centurion replied, "Lord, I do not deserve to have you come under my roof. But just say the word, and my servant will be healed. For I myself am a man under authority, with soldiers under me. I tell this one, 'Go,' and he goes; and that one, 'Come,' and he comes. I say to my servant, 'Do this,' and he does it." When Jesus heard this, he was astonished and said to those following him, "I tell you the truth, I have not found anyone in Israel with such great faith."

Then Jesus said to the centurion, "Go! It will be done just as you believed it would." And his servant was healed at that very hour."[16]

I just think it is interesting that Jesus says that understanding authority is actually a display of great faith.

Let me say that again.

Understanding authority is a display of great faith.

As warriors, we are to yield to authority, and there are plenty of earthly examples of authority we can yield to.

As well as a heavenly one.

And as warriors we must understand that if we are yielded to authority, then we have been given authority.

If we are going to win the battles of our life, we must walk in the authority we have as children of the King.

So, who is the "boss of you"?

chapter 9

ready or not . . .

This youngest son always carried two things: a sling and a small guitarlike instrument.

Spare time for a sheep-herder is abundant on rich mountain plateaus where sheep can graze for days in one sequestered meadow.

But as time passed and days became weeks, the young man became very lonely.

The feeling of friendlessness that always roamed inside him was magnified.

He played his harp a great deal.

He had a good voice, so he often sang.

When these activities failed to comfort him, he gathered up a pile of stones and, one by one, swung them at a distant tree with something akin to fury.

When one rock pile was depleted, he would walk to the blistered tree, reassemble his rocks, and designate another leafy enemy at yet a farther distance.

He engaged in many such solitary battles.

When not occupied with his flock, he swung his companionable sling and swung it again and again until he could tell every rock precisely where to go.

One day, with a song of praise on his lips, he froze. He spied a real enemy, a breathing threat to his flock. Both the bear and the boy were fixated on the helpless lamb between them. Dark eyes of furry madness met the trusting eyes of a determined youth. Instinctively reaching for his sling and his stone, the boy paused to realize, "Why, I am not afraid."

The bear charged at the shepherd with foaming madness.

The young man took a smooth pebble, put it in his leather sling and launched it at his furry enemy.

His aim was dead on.

The young shepherd was victorious.

The bear defeated.[1]

His daily training with the pebbles had saved the little lamb's life.

One day, his practice with those pebbles would save the army of Israel.

It is the unseen battles that make the warrior.

David's time in the sheep pen—aiming at trees, killing the bear and praise becoming his battle cry—is what made him able to stand before Goliath.

Unafraid, he faced the giant.

And won.

It is the strength he built when no one was watching that helped him to stand in Saul's courts and face a king gone mad.

If we are to be warriors, we must commit to training. That includes doing the right thing over and over and over until it becomes habit. Things like loving people, being health conscious, being alert and watchful, stretching our capacity—and so much more.

There is a lot to be said about a properly trained warrior.

I heard one of the actors in the movie *Black Hawk Down* tell of his experiences. He was going to be portraying a Marine and so decided

138   chapter 9

to spend some time before the filming began with a squad of Marines. He said he had no idea what was involved in being a Marine and he had just thought that all Marines were naturally heroic. But after spending weeks with them, he said that what they were was prepared. They trained over and over and over and over so that when in a battle situation they knew exactly what to do. Their responses became instinct.

Hero status was a natural by-product of instinct.

And instinct is developed in the unseen preparation of a warrior.

When taking karate, I learned to do katas, or forms. Basically these were imaginary fights with multiple opponents. If done well, a kata not only looked like a dance but was also a series of powerful moves. Over the years on my black-belt journey, I had to learn many of these forms. The closer I got to the black-belt test, the more difficult the forms became. I spent hours and hours and hours practicing the 16 forms that comprised my big test. I prac-ticed so much that my muscles knew what to do even if my mind had a blank moment.

Which turned out to be a good thing.

Because I did have a "zone out" moment during the course of the four-hour test.

But because I had practiced *so* much, my muscle memory kicked in and carried me until my brain reengaged!

I have heard it said that a thought determines an action. An action determines a habit, and a habit determines our future. So what we do over and over and over determines where we will go and how we will act in the tough times.

One of the Navy SEAL maxims is, "Training remains strict to enforce the belief that the more you sweat in peacetime, the less you will bleed in war."

Even the Girl Scout motto is "Be prepared."

If we are going to be successful warriors, we had better be prepared. And preparation requires training.

> **Train** [treyn]: *verb*
> -to develop or form the habits, thoughts, or behavior by discipline and instruction:
> -to make proficient by instruction and practice, as in some art, profession, or work[2]

My daughter Paris and I really, really want a little puppy—the kind that stays little for a lifetime, like a Pekapoo or a Shippoo.

I know.

Very weird names.

But *very* cute dogs!!

However, as exciting as a new puppy would be, training it might not be so exciting . . . especially considering our new, very wool, very hard to clean carpet.

Much like a newborn, the puppy will not know that it can't take care of business any time, any place. Plus, last time I checked, they do not make puppy diapers. And really, until I am a grandmother, I am finished with the diaper phase of my life!

We are committed to training our puppy to go outside to do his business. We have gotten advice from professional trainers and read some books. We have bought the supplies, and we are ready to invest the time needed. We will show him over and over and over what it is that we want him to do. Through discipline and instruction, we will train him in what to do.

I am sure there will be some mistakes along the way. And it would be pretty silly for Paris or myself to beat the puppy every time he has an accident. He will be learning, so extra grace will be required on our part. (Shoot!)

Can I suggest that while we are training (which will be for the rest of our lives), we offer this grace not just to puppies and newborns, but also to ourselves?

In life, we will fumble. Even when we are fully engaged, we will make mistakes. Even if our heart is after God's, we will face our own limitations. Maybe in God's eyes, we are not much different from the little puppy. He knows we are doing our best to train for eternity.

Michael Jordan is one of the greatest basketball players to ever have played the game. He played with passion, with purpose, with all he had. And this is what he said: "I've missed more than 9,000 shots in my career. I've lost almost 300 games. Twenty-six times, I've been trusted to take the game winning shot and missed. I've failed over and over and over again in my life. And that is why I succeed."[3]

Training doesn't guarantee that we will never fail. But it does guarantee that we will get back up and do the right thing.

The prophet Jeremiah was basically whining to God about the condition of his life, how hard it was, how unfair things were. God challenged him, saying, "So, Jeremiah, if you're worn out in this footrace with men, what makes you think you can race against horses? And if you can't keep your wits during times of calm, what's going to happen when troubles break loose like the Jordan in flood?"[4] Basically God was saying, "Hey, Jeremiah, if this is hard for you today, how are you going to handle it when it gets even more difficult? Will you make it then? This time you are going through now is basically training for the real battle, so you better get through this one, or the real battle might end up destroying you."

The Bible promises that if we train up a child in the way he should go, then in his old age, he will not depart from it.[5]

What way do you want your children going? Then train them that way.

Show them over and over again.

Demonstrate with your own life what you want them to do.

My children are not perfect.

In fact, I have failed in teaching my son how to do any household tasks. He is about to move into his own home, and it will be interesting to watch him do the basics involved in running a house. Maybe we should have a crash course, or at least I could buy him a DVD on housework for dummies.

I have also failed in teaching my daughter how to cook. Okay, she can make scrambled eggs and toast and cereal. But really, how many years can she live on breakfast?

So, I admit it, there are certain areas in which I have failed to train my children.

But there are some areas of training that we did do right.

They know how to dress themselves.

They take showers.

They are potty trained.

They chew with their mouths closed (most of the time).

They rarely burp at the table.

They know how to make a decision.

They know how to pray.

Both of them love God.

They love His house.

They love serving in His house.

They love each other.

They love their parents.

They are committed to finding and fulfilling God's will in their lives.

They are learning that they are entitled to nothing. That they must work hard to see the dreams of their heart birthed. They are learning that God is only obligated to see His dream fulfilled in their lives—not to fulfill any selfish desires they may have.

> **Train** [treyn]: *verb*
> -to make (a person) fit by proper exercise, diet, practice[6]

This sounds like fun, doesn't it?

Warriors are committed to being fit.

Why?

So that we have a shot at winning the battle.

For years I think I was just ignorant of the fact that I have an obligation to be as healthy as possible.

That there is a generation counting on me to hand them a baton.

And that I need to take care of the only body I have been given so that I can finish my race strong.

For years I abused my body, thinking that it would just bounce back. And for years it did.

I would hear about healthy eating from time to time, but never really applied what I learned.

It just seemed too hard.

And certainly not convenient.

Well.

Getting cancer was harder.

And definitely more inconvenient.

So now, I was willing to learn what it takes to get and stay healthy.

To take care of the body that God has entrusted me with.

I learned what true health is.

Of course, Dr. Myron Wentz helped me out a little with this:

> True health is not simply how you feel when you wake up each morning. Nor is it a favorable lab, radiology, or physical exam report from your physician. True health is not based on the sculpture of your physique nor your ability to compete in a triathlon. True health is being absolutely the best you can be with the conditions you were given and situation in which you now live. True health is not just the absence of disease. It is empowering our bodies to perform at their optimum level.
>
> [Optimal health is] energy and stamina . . . flexibility, strength and endurance. Optimal health means having reserves to deal with the unexpected stresses encountered in everyday life. It includes having a clear, strong mind and a good memory. It means having a feeling of spiritual harmony and balance. It means looking forward to every new day, not looking back at the good old days. Good health cannot and must not be taken for granted. It should be guarded, with utmost security and attention, every day of our lives. That is the most effective way to avoid degenerative disease and thus to achieve the maximum number of years of active, enjoyable living. Only by maintaining good health can we do what we want to do and need to do for ourselves and our loved ones.[7]

I learned that fewer Americans are dying of contagious diseases and more are dying from degenerative ones.

I learned that the fuel we put into our bodies—not to mention how we deal with our toxic environment—matters.

I finally heard what the U.S. Surgeon General said more than 15 years ago. He said, "What we eat may affect our risk for several of the leading causes of death for Americans, notably, coronary heart disease, stroke, atherosclerosis, diabetes, and some types of cancer. These disorders together now account for more than two-thirds of all deaths in the United States."[8]

I started taking Proverbs 31:17 personally: "She girds herself with strength [spiritual, mental and physical fitness for her God-given task] and makes her arms strong and firm."[9]

I truly realized that I have a responsibility to do my part to stay healthy.

I felt challenged enough to change when I heard Paul confront the Corinthians: "But, [like a boxer] I buffet my body [handle it roughly, discipline it by hardships] and subdue it, for fear that after proclaiming to others the Gospel and things pertaining to it, I myself should become unfit [not stand the test, be unapproved and rejected as a counterfeit]."[10]

I read dozens of books.

And I made changes so that I could be fit.

I trained.

So I changed what I ate.

When I slept.

How I exercised.

I became committed to being strong.

I am asking you to do the same.

No.

I am begging you.

Please commit to getting fit.

We need you.

Warriors are alert to the times and to what is going on around them.

By his own words, Gideon calls himself the weakest in his weak family. He does not see his potential.

He just feels unqualified.

Have you ever felt like that?

Like everyone else is a better choice than you are?

God loves using weak and humble people. He has done it for centuries.

God sees Gideon hiding out from the enemy and sends an angel to him.

The angel greets him, "Hey, mighty man!"

I bet Gideon looked over his shoulder. Surely the angel was not talking to him.

The angel tells Gideon that he himself will lead the Israelites in victory over their oppressors.

Gideon thinks this is crazy talk.

His family is weak and he is the youngest.

He is convinced that God has the wrong guy and so asks for some confirmation.

He gets it.

Now he has a battle to prepare for.

He gathers all the men. They number 32,000 in total. Not a bad number. But still a little small when they know that the enemy numbers over 135,000.

But God took a look at Gideon's army and told him it was too big.

Too big!

Was God kidding?

Even if they each killed four of the enemy, that still wouldn't be enough.

But God had a plan.

So he told Gideon to tell all those who were afraid to go home.

And 22,000 said, "Thanks, I am out of here!"

Now the army was down to 10,000.

I am sure that Gideon was wondering what God was up to.

God decided that the army was still too large.

So He sent them all to the water to get a drink.

And 9,700 of them stuck their faces in the water to drink.

Only 300 stood and brought the water to their faces.

God told Gideon to send the 9,700 home.[11]

Why?

Because, while tending to their natural needs, they forgot to be alert to what was going on around them. They were not looking for an enemy or any other threat. They were too focused on what they needed.

By the way, even outnumbered 450 to 1, the Israelites defeated their enemy. (Well, sort of outnumbered—they did have one very powerful God on their side!)

Certainly 300 alert, courageous warriors are better than an army of 32,000 distracted soldiers.

We have got to be alert to what is going on around us. Probably like me, you have seen those commercials challenging parents to talk to their children. They usually start out with, "Do you know where your child is?" or "Do you know who is talking to your children about drugs/alcohol/sex?"

The point being that we should be alert to the world in which our children live. It is not easy. And sometimes talking to them is just inconvenient and might be uncomfortable.

The brain of a teenager works far differently from an adult's.

That is obvious.

In fact, studies have shown that their brains are almost dead early in the morning but are seriously alive in the later evening.

Just when mine is shutting down!

But I have to be alert—to take care of my needs while being aware of my kids' needs. So, I have had *many* late night conversations with my teenagers about so many things. Most of the time I would have rather been sleeping, but I knew if I stayed awake and listened, I would learn much about what was going on in their world.

There have also been moments when, because I do my best to be alert to the quiet voice of the Spirit of God, I have prayed for my children. I remember many times, as I was going about my day, that I just sensed that right there, in that moment, I needed to pray for them.

So I did.

For protection, wisdom or favor . . . sometimes all three!

Jesus told His disciples to watch and pray.

Watch and pray.

Watch. Keep on the lookout for what is going on.

Pray. Talk to God about what you are seeing.

Be alert for what is going on in your world now.

Do you need to spend some time with your children?

How about your husband?

Do you have a friend who could really use some of your time?

Do you need to spend some time praying?

How about getting information on how to live a healthy lifestyle?

Is this the time to take your company in a different direction?

Is this the time to change jobs?

Warriors need to know what season they're in.

In Southern California, we don't really get to experience the seasons. Palm trees don't change colors, and I have yet to build a snowman in my front yard. Basically we live in perpetual spring and summer. And I love that!

However, those of you who live elsewhere are much better at preparing for seasons.

You have learned to be alert to the indicators that a new season is coming.

You pull the lawn furniture in and winterize (whatever that is!) the garden.

You get the snow shovel and the rake out from under the pool toys. You bring the coats up from the basement.

You are alert to a coming season change.

If you live in Florida or along the Atlantic coast, during the summer and fall months you keep alert for hurricanes. And if warned, you batten down the hatch or evacuate. Those who haven't been alert have often paid for their lack of vigilance.

The apostle Peter challenges us to be well balanced and vigilant because our enemy is seeking someone to devour.[12]

> **Vig-i-lant** [vij-*uh*-l*uh*nt] -ever awake and alert; sleeplessly watchful[13]

I don't think this means that we can't ever take a nap.

But I do think it means that if we want to be victorious, we must be vigilant . . . ever watchful. We must be aware of what's going on around us.

I am sure you have seen the police shows on television where an officer is on a stakeout.

The officer has to be alert and ready to catch the criminal he is waiting for.

I am sure that in the dark, quiet moments it would be easy to fall asleep.

I am sure that there are moments when the officer suspects that the criminal is not coming.

I am sure there are moments when he just wants to leave.

What if he does?

What if he falls asleep?

Maybe you are on a "stakeout."

There are times we all are.

Don't get distracted.

Don't fall asleep.

Don't leave.

Life is not without stress.

Daily we will face stressful situations.

And they won't all go away.

So how we handle the stress is really what is important.

During my two-week hospital stay, one of the doctors performed a test that measured my stress level. Before the test began, he asked me how stressed I was feeling. I told them that I felt fine. He hooked me up to a machine and did the test.

The results shocked me.

He said that my stress level indicated that at that moment I was staring a roaring lion in the face.

A roaring lion.

In the face.

And the shocking thing was—I had no idea.

Obviously I needed to get better at recognizing and handling stress!

One of the jobs on my résumé is "Professional Plate Spinner." Within that job is my capacity to be a wife, mother, pastor, teacher, author, friend, leader—you get the idea! I spin lots of plates. And I bet you do, too.

But I did not start out spinning all these plates at once.

Nope.

I just got good at one and then another was added.

And then another.

And then another.

As my capacity increased, so did the number of plates.

Well, that ought to teach me to pray the prayer of Jabez!

He prayed that God would bless him and increase his territory.

God did.

He is always about increase.

Warriors are ever increasing their capacity.

I have learned that enlarging my territory means enlarging my area of responsibility.

I think God needs us to be great at handling more.

Not running in lanes we shouldn't, but great at handling all that is within our own lane.

The King of heaven is counting on us to do our part, which definitely involves growing and stretching.

When the prophet Nehemiah was rebuilding the wall of Jerusalem, not everyone was happy about it. Many of the workers had to have a brick in one hand and a sword in another. They were not just builders, but builders and warriors. Managing more than one plate.

Jesus told a story about a man who went on a trip. Before he left, he got his three servants together and gave $5,000 to one, $2,000 to another and $1,000 to the third. He gave each an amount based on his ability to handle it. The one who had been given the $5,000 wisely invested it, and it doubled. The one who had been given $2,000 also doubled his money. However, the man with $1,000 buried his money in the ground and did nothing with it. The employer came back and rewarded the two who doubled what they had been given. He then became angry with the one who had not tried to grow or increase what had been given to him. So, the employer took the $1,000 away from him.[14]

Each man was given resources based on his particular capacity. Not because the owner was playing favorites.

Sometimes we ask God for more, and if He did give us more, we wouldn't be able to contain it because we don't have the capacity. I have read stories of people who have won millions of dollars in the lottery, and yet in a few years they have lost most of it because they didn't have the capacity to handle millions.[15]

As a parent, I have never given my kids more than they can handle. They always *wanted* more than they could handle. But I never would have given my car keys to my daughter when she was 10, no matter how many times she asked.

Why?

Is it because I was a mean mother?

No.

I knew she would hurt herself and others if she had gotten behind the wheel then. She didn't have the ability to drive a car then. Now, as a 15-year-old, her capacity has increased, and with supervision and a permit (yikes!), she can drive the car.

Jesus said if we were faithful with little, He would make us ruler over much.

We all want the "much."

It's the "being faithful with little" that is hard.

"Being faithful with little" to receiving the "much" doesn't happen overnight.

Michael Jordan's going from not making his high school basketball team to the greatest player ever was not an overnight process.

There were thousands of days and millions of basketball shots that separated the two realities.

Training requires dedication.

Dedication to the end result.

I knew that in order for me to get healthy, it was going to take more than eating one salad.

I had to make drastic health changes.

Like throwing out everything in my pantry in one day.

I had to switch gears mentally and then switch them physically.

That meant shopping at new stores (where they sell very strange natural products).

Cooking organic foods.

Learning about juicing veggies.

Planting wheatgrass.

Swallowing 70-plus horse pills a day.

Reading stacks of health books.

Exercising every morning (*every* morning!).

And taking my family and friends along for the journey.

It makes me dizzy thinking about it!

What can distract us today is that we live in a microwave society. Everything is instant: fast food, mail orders, emails, cell phones, travel. Even our pharmacies are drive-thru! We want it when we want it, and we want it right *now*!

Our celebrity culture influences us to think that we can live the "high life" (what is that anyway?) without any effort or discipline on our part. We subscribe to an entitlement mentality and pursue life with an attitude that says, "I deserve to have all my dreams come true just because I want them to."

But the real high life does not consist of endless achievements, worthless goal setting and people pleasing. It's all about a life rooted in God. It is knowing who you are in Him, knowing the purpose for which you have been created and staying committed to working that out.

Day in and day out.

Rain or shine.

When it's easy and when it's not.

Sometimes, we look at the lives of those who have gone before us and who achieved greatness, and we want in 5 minutes what took them 25 years of unseen work to build!

Training takes time.

No athlete competing in the Olympics got there with one training session.

No champion ice skater got there with one spin on the ice.

No CEO got there the first day on the job.

No mother became an expert with the first diaper change.

The writer of Hebrews encourages us to run with patient endurance and steady and active persistence the appointed course of the race that has been set before us.[16]

The word here that is translated as "race" comes from the Greek word *agon*. And it is from the word *agon* that we get the word "agony."

Why is this important to know? Because the race you and I are running, the race for victory, is not a casual Sunday afternoon jog;

rather, it is a difficult and often agonizing race. It will take determination and training to finish.

We shouldn't get frustrated at our low-paying job. If we are faithful to be the best employee in this job, and our capacity is increasing, then we might be able to handle a bigger and better job.

And this increase in capacity must take place in every aspect of our life.

I should be increasing my capacity to love.

I should be increasing my capacity to forgive.

I should be increasing my capacity to write books.

I should be increasing my message-writing capacity.

I should be increasing my capacity to give.

I should be increasing my vision.

And if I am going to do all of that increasing, then I must spend time with people who have an even bigger capacity than mine.

People who love more.

People who forgive more.

People who write more books.

People who are more effective teachers.

People who are more generous givers.

People with a more profound vision.

Yep, I am spinning lots of plates.

And, yes, sometimes I have some painful "stretch" moments.

But you know what?

God is not looking down at me and feeling sorry for me.

He is looking way ahead.

He sees the place where I am going and knows that I need to be enlarging, so He is saying, "Come on, Holly! Get good at what is in your life now because I have so much more for you. I have people farther up the road whom I need you to touch . . . so keep growing!"

Only those who will increase their capacity, who will be stretched willingly, will be promoted through the ranks.

It is these who make history.

> For who is God except the Lord?
>
> Who but our God is a solid rock?
>
> God arms me with strength
>
> and he makes my way perfect.
>
> He makes me as surefooted as a deer,
>
> enabling me to stand on mountain heights.
>
> He trains my hands for battle;
>
> he strengthens my arm to draw a bronze.
>
> Psalm 18:31-34, *NLT*

chapter 10

more than

At one time or another, we have *all* been victims of something.

From the "not so big a deal" to "the devastating."

What is a victim? The *American Heritage Dictionary* calls a victim "one who is harmed or made to suffer; a person who is tricked, swindled or taken advantage of."[1]

I have looked at pictures of me from the 1980s.

What was I thinking?

Definite fashion victim.

Tricked by the fashion industry into thinking those leggings looked good.

I was also a victim of thinking I had to be like someone else. I wasted a lot of time trying to look and act like someone else. Basically I was trying to run in a lane that wasn't mine. Someone else's lane always looked like more fun!

Many have been a victim of someone else's narrow mind.

Of someone's hatred.

Most of us have been a victim of some kind of discrimination.

Because of the color of our skin.

The money, or lack of it, in our bank account.

Our level of education.

The wheelchair.

The accent.

Our gender.

We are all, to some degree, victims of our upbringing.

Many of us have been a victim of child abuse.

Or a victim of an alcoholic, angry parent.

Or a victim of clueless parents who did not understand that parenting is about giving.

Maybe one of your parents died when you were young.

Maybe you were the victim of abandonment.

Maybe one of your family members was murdered.

Some of us have been the victims of a violent crime. Some of us have been the victim of a rape or mugging.

There are many of us who have been the victims of a vicious disease.

Some of us have perhaps been victims of anorexia or bulimia.

I have traveled to quite a few developing nations and seen thousands of victims of absolute poverty.

Some of you might be victims of fear or perhaps just timidity.

So you avoid things.

And now fear has opened the door to more fear. Now you are locked in a cage of fear.

Being a victim is heartbreaking.

Hearing stories of victims makes me cry.

Now, we must begin the sometimes long journey out.

The journey out of being a victim.

I am not saying it will be easy.

I am not saying it will be without pain.

And we will need other warriors to help us.

But we can do it.

We can.

Most victims ask, "Why? Why me?"

Sometimes people get so comfortable with their status as a victim that that is how they see themselves.

The goal, however, is not to stay a victim.

The goal is to move from victim to survivor.

From survivor to overcomer.

Warriors make the journey.

A lot of people still see themselves as victims. As victims many of us get lots of compassion and love.

Which brings about healing.

The problem is when the sympathy that can begin the healing process becomes the sympathy that hinders. It becomes the sympathy that keeps us a victim. We fear losing the love that we receive as victims.

Not good.

There will come a time when we must realize that it is time to move on.

We must choose to move from victim to survivor; and it will take motivation.

I heard a story of a man who was walking through a cemetery on his way home one night. He accidentally fell into a newly dug, empty grave (gross!). He tried over and over again to get out, but he was unsuccessful. So he settled down to wait for morning. Later that night, another man walked through the cemetery and also fell into the grave (get it, don't walk through cemeteries at night!). He desperately tried to get out, unaware that there was anyone else in the grave. The first man listened to the second man struggle for a few minutes, and then spoke to him out of the darkness, "You can't get out of here." But you know what? All of a sudden, he did.

He had the motivation!

If you and I are going to move from being a victim to being a survivor, we must have the motivation.

A survivor is someone who remains alive, having coped with a trauma or setback.

We have probably all sung along with Gloria Gaynor as she belted out, "I will survive!"

Come on, admit it!

Choosing to survive takes a strong decision, motivation and courage.

We must choose not to let the situation or the circumstance destroy us.

I cried during a scene in the movie *Paradise Road* in which a few of the women could no longer endure their captivity. They had survived for a few years, but when moved to a new prison camp, they decided that they couldn't survive another day. They just lay down on their pallets and chose to die. Survival was too hard.

So, yes, it takes courage to survive.

Sometimes pure guts.

Maybe you have gone through a divorce.

Yes, it was hurtful.

Yes, you wanted to stay in your bed and eat Häagen Dazs.

But you didn't.

You got on with your life.

You chose to survive.

Maybe a close friend betrayed you.

It broke your heart.

You thought it best to just withdraw from people.

But you didn't.

You made another friend.

You chose to survive.

You survived high school.

A rough patch in your marriage.

A health crisis.

Your child's toddler years.

Her teen years.

And you did it because you made a decision to survive.

Surviving takes gaining knowledge.

To survive cancer, I had to gain knowledge. I did not just yield my health to a team of doctors.

I learned some things about health, nutrition, and treatment options.

I read books and went to seminars.

To survive troubled times in my marriage, I had to gain some knowledge.

About men.

About the differences between men and women.

About how to communicate respect.

To survive my son's teenaged years (and so that he would too!), I had to gain some knowledge.

About boundaries.

About young men.

About appropriate discipline.

In many cases, surviving takes humbling ourselves and admitting that some of what we are choosing to survive . . . well, we caused in the first place.

Obviously, I am not talking to those of you who have experienced abuse. You are not at fault for what happened. Let me say it again. It is not your fault. It only becomes your fault if you refuse to deal with it and choose to bring it into your future.

But maybe some of us have lived an unhealthy lifestyle, so now we have a sickness we have to survive.

Or we had an affair, so now our marriage is in serious trouble.

Perhaps we lied, so now we have lost the trust of people we care about.

Or we weren't diligent at work, so now our job is on the line.

Remember, victims ask, "Why?"

Well, survivors ask, "What?"

What can I do to get through this?

What do I need to learn?

What should I do differently?

Surviving is good.

It means you haven't been defeated.

Many of you have survived traumatic childhoods. And you can look back and say, "Man, it is a miracle that I survived that." And it is.

For me, surviving cancer was good. Definitely beats the alternative!

We all might do different things to survive the situation in which we find ourselves.

We might eat chocolate—a lot of it.

We might cry—often.

We might go to a counselor.

We might hide.

In order to survive, some victims of child abuse have just blocked it out, refusing to allow it into their conscious thoughts. Others intentionally become overweight so that they are no longer attractive to men. Some just live in anger.

All of these are acceptable when we're in survival mode.

Because we definitely want to survive.

But we will need to do things differently if we want to take the next step.

And because we are warriors, we *will* take the next step.

The step of becoming an overcomer.

We become an overcomer when we are focused on helping others, when we are not concerned just about our own survival anymore. Now we are extending our hand to someone else. We are taking what we have learned and are using it to help another.

Honestly, this is what it is all about.

This is why we *must* move from victim to overcomer.

This is one of the most important journeys you and I will make.

And I think God is waiting.

He is waiting for us to be able to take our eyes off ourselves and see someone else who is hurting.

Victims ask, "Why?"

Survivors ask, "What?"

Overcomers ask, "Who and how?"

"Who can I help? And how can I help them?"

Many people around the world have experienced the devastation of flooding.

Many people were victims, in the United States and in Southeast Asia, as their homes, their cities, were overtaken by water.

Some survived.

They grabbed hold of a tree and hung on.

They climbed into a boat, grateful to be there.

Some were overcomers.

While they were clinging to the tree with one hand, they extended the other to bring someone else to the safety of the tree.

When they were securely in the boat, they reached out and pulled others into the boat as well.

Overcomers.

Immaculee Ilibagiza grew up in a country she loved.

She thought it was paradise.

She was surrounded by a family she adored, and who adored her.

In 1994 her peaceful world was destroyed as Rwanda became embroiled in bloody genocide.

The war ultimately claimed the lives of nearly one million Rwandans.

It was a miracle that Immaculee survived the slaughter.

For 91 days, she and 7 other women hid in a bathroom.

Four feet long and three feet wide.

A bathroom.

Ninety-one days.

Seven women.

They took turns standing up and stretching.

They would go days without food and water.

They had to maintain absolute silence.

They couldn't say a word.

Not one.

Because there were crazed killers looking for them.

Killers who had been neighbors.

Killers who had been friends.

At any moment those killers might search the home of the pastor who was hiding them.

The killers did come to search the house.

Many times.

It was a miracle they were not discovered.

She could hear through the window the slaughter of the innocent outside. She could hear the cry of babies.

After seven weeks in the bathroom, the women were nothing but skin and bones.

They suffered from body lice and painful infections.

There was no medicine.

But it was during those hours of unimaginable terror that Immaculee discovered prayer and a new, life-changing relationship with God.

For weeks, she wrestled with anger, fear and the pain of betrayal.

When she eventually left the bathroom for the relative safety of a refugee camp, she had discovered the meaning of unconditional love—a love so strong and so real that she was able to forgive her family's killers.

She could forgive them.

Those who had murdered her family.

Now she is working on establishing a foundation to help others heal from the long-term effects of genocide and war.

She was a victim.

She survived.

Now she is an overcomer . . . helping others survive.

Read her story in her book *Left to Tell*.[2]

Overcomers see past their victimization.

Past just "surviving."

They see others that need help.

To become an overcomer we have to realize that we have been created to be an overcomer.

The apostle Paul put it like this: "Yet amid all these things we are <u>more than conquerors</u> and gain a surpassing victory through Him Who loved us."[3]

Amid all what things?

Oh, just little things like suffering and affliction and tribulation and calamity and distress and persecution and hunger and destitution and peril and the sword.[4]

We are more than conquerors *in* all these things—in challenges, trials and battles. Not in spite of them . . . but in the midst of them.

In all these things.

I know some people who *love* to surf.

They travel around the world looking for the big waves.

I have seen photos and videos of them surfing giant waves.

The kind of waves I would be afraid to swim in.

Just the photos scare me!

Yep, the surf that freaks out an ordinary swimmer like me absolutely thrills the surfer.

In the midst of the giant waves, they are more than conquerors.

On the journey toward being an overcomer, we have to get great at forgetting the past and reaching forward.

In his letter to the Philippians, Paul said that while he hadn't learned everything, he had certainly gotten good at forgetting those things that are behind and reaching forward to those things that are ahead.[5]

What does it mean to forget our past?

I am certainly not suggesting that we all develop amnesia. I *am* suggesting that we let go of any baggage from our yesterdays that we are dragging into our today.

Yes, you were a victim.

Yes, bad things happened to you.

Please deal with the stuff in your heart so that you can become an overcomer.

Forgive.

Let go.

You will never be able to change your past.

You will never be able to change what happened to you.

But you do have the power to create your future.

A future unhindered by the pain of yesterday.

But only if you want it.

Forgetting closes the door to our past and reaching ahead opens the door to our future.

One time I went in a jewelry store that had two consecutive doors.

After entering the first one, I stood in a small area until the door closed behind me. The next door would not open until the first door had closed.

It is the same for you and me.

Our future is before us.

We won't be able to enter the door of our future until we have closed the door to our past.

There are some things in us that must be dealt with before we can move on . . .

Before Paul had his encounter with Jesus, he did some terrible things. He had some forgetting to do.

He had to forget that on *his* orders Stephen, a young Christian, had been stoned to death . . . while he stood and watched.

He was a murderer.

Could you forget that?

If Paul hadn't learned to deal with his past, he'd never have written half of the New Testament or helped establish a church that would last millenniums.

We must put a period on the past.

The book of Joshua opens with God reminding Joshua that Moses was dead.

I am sure Joshua knew it.

In his head.

Maybe he was just a little freaked out in his heart.

So God said, "Moses is dead. Now get up and go—cross the Jordan."

I just wonder.

Maybe Joshua didn't feel like he was ready for Moses' job.

He had served him for over 40 years.

He was comfortable in that role.

Now he had to leave behind the familiar. But why?

Because he would not have been able to lead the people into their future if he had not let go of the past.

In the past the children of Israel had been nomads . . . wanderers.

In their future they were to be settlers, taking up residence in the land of promise.

In the past they had eaten daily manna.

In the future, they were to sow seeds, reap harvests. Occupy the land.

Joshua had to let go of the past in order to walk into the future.

Even though he was probably afraid.

As an overcomer, we can't look back.

We have to reach toward the life of promise.

Lot, his wife and his daughters lived in Sodom.

Not a great place to live.

It was such a foul place that God was about to destroy it.

He sent angels to lead Lot and his family out.

There was just one condition.

As they were leaving, they couldn't look back.

They were to look toward their future.

Maybe Lot's wife got sentimental about what she was leaving.

Because she looked back and turned into a pillar of salt.

She became crystallized—as a person who couldn't let go of the past.

An overcomer is someone who uses his or her past to give someone else a future.

The apostle Paul told us that God comes alongside us when we go through hard times, and before we know it, He brings us alongside someone else who is going through hard times so that we can be there for that person just as God has been there for us.[6]

In my marriage we have made this journey.

We were definitely victims—Philip was from a broken home and had experienced a failed marriage.

And we were both victims of trials in our own marriage.

But we made it through the challenges.

We survived.

Now we help other couples with their marriages.

Overcomers.

I was a victim of cancer.

I learned some things so that I could survive.

One person told me that I really needed to live in the mountains.

Somewhere with clean air and no stress.

For a minute I was tempted.

But doing that would just be surviving.

And I was created to be an overcomer.

So I would live in the city God put me in and fulfill my purpose, helping people all along the way.

Overcoming always involves living on purpose and with purpose!

We are all trusted with the spotlight, whether big or small.

It is never so that we can just selfishly shine brighter, but so that our light can help someone else out of the dark.

As a victim . . . you were in the dark.

As a survivor . . . you see a light at the end of the tunnel—so you get through.

As an overcomer . . . you become the light for someone else.

Just like my friend Harmony.

When she was just a year old, her mother and father divorced. Both parents struggled with drug addictions.

When she was three, she was exposed to pornography.

When she was five, she was molested by two women.

When she was seven, she was molested by an older boy.

When she was eight, her drug-addict mother was almost killed by a man who broke into their home and beat her with brass knuckles.

When she was 13, her mother's boyfriend began pursuing her sexually. She started running away from home. The boyfriend moved out and her mom followed him, leaving her alone with her 8-year-old brother for 3 months.

When she was 14, she was raped by her ex-boyfriend. More than once. In fact, so many times that she stopped fighting him. As a result of the attacks, she was kicked out of school for having sex on campus. The school staff made an announcement over the PA system, telling everyone why she had been kicked out. The rumor around school was that she was having an orgy and filming a porno movie in the auditorium. Her reputation had been formed and followed her all the way to college.

When she was 16, her boyfriend was shot in the head. She tried to cut her wrists.

When she was 19, some guy at college told her that she should become a stripper to solve her financial problems. She didn't want to.

She made an appointment with one of her psychology professors to seek advice. She looked up to him and hoped he would tell her not to do it. He said, "You might as well do it. It's not like you have to add it to your résumé."

So she began stripping. While still going to school, she worked as an assistant teacher by day and a stripper by night. She finally ended up quitting her day job. Her psychology professor came to the club and had one of his friends ask her to do a table dance for him. She was finally convinced that all men were sick and perverted.

Her boyfriend got another girl pregnant. The pregnant girl moved in with them.

When she was 20, she started sleeping with women. One of her girlfriends moved in with her, her boyfriend and the boyfriend's other girlfriend!

When she was 21, she met a girl in ballet class and developed a friendship. This girl invited her to church. She went. She encountered a love that took her breath away, and she pursued a relationship with God. She began to understand her worth and value. She went to recovery classes and Bible studies. She quit stripping.

When she was 23, she graduated with a B.A. in psychology.

When she was 26, she married a man who adored her, who treated her with the love and dignity any daughter of the King should know.

When she was 27, she started a master's degree program. And she started a group called Treasures out of Darkness. This group of girls from our church goes into the strip clubs, taking gifts to the dancers and demonstrating the love of God. Many of the dancers, upon encountering Harmony and the girls of Treasures, begin the journey toward understanding their value. Many have left the club life.

Harmony was a victim of so much pain that it breaks my heart.

She survived.

Now she is an overcomer.

In the very arena in which the enemy tried to destroy her, she is now leading others to freedom.

I love that.

Victim.

Survivor.

Overcomer.

Who you were.

Who you are.

Who you are destined to be.

chapter 11

braveheart

Her life had been a difficult one.

Her husband had been murdered.

She was trying to overcome an addiction to methamphetamines.

Someone else was raising her daughter.

She really wanted a different life.

She wanted to start over.

So, she opened her Bible once again.

She began to hope.

She started reading a book called *The Purpose Driven Life*.

She began to see that her life did have meaning.

One day a man named Brian Nichols barged into her home, holding her hostage.

He had just killed a man and wounded others.

The police were looking for him.

She was scared, not knowing if he would kill her or not.

She started talking to him about her daughter and her family.

She asked him about his life.

In spite of her fear, she made him breakfast.

She read to him from *The Purpose Driven Life*.

She started to wonder whether Brian's being in her home wasn't a part of some master plan.

He wanted her to explain what she had read—about what it means to have a purpose.

She shared the love of God with him.

The one holding a gun on her.

She saw him as a person.

Wow.

She kept talking to him about her need to go see her daughter.

She said that she did not want him to hurt anyone else.

He said he didn't either.

He let her go.

He surrendered to a SWAT team.

Ashley Smith's courage saved her life and the lives of others.

And perhaps it opened heaven's door to a man who needed to encounter God.[1]

She was married to a fool.

Really.

Why would her parents choose a fool for her to marry?

That was his name, Nabal . . . which means "fool."

And he was living up to the name his parents gave him.

Her life can't have been an easy one.

This story begins at the time of sheep shearing.

The time of abundance.

Parties.

David, before he officially became king, and his 600 followers were hiding from King Saul.

While they were hiding, they had been protecting Nabal's herdsmen (unbeknownst to Nabal).

When David and his men were low on provisions, David sent 10 men to give greetings to Nabal and to ask for some food.

This was not an unreasonable request.

It was feast time, and he had protected Nabal's herdsmen.

Nabal, probably drunk, rejected the greeting from David and refused to share any food. He told the men to "get out of here!"

Not smart.

He just rejected David.

This is *the* David—the one God fights for.

Sure enough, when David heard of Nabal's rejection, he told his men to strap on their swords.

It was going to be war.

Meanwhile, back at the ranch, one of Nabal's servants said to Abigail, "You are not going to believe this! Your husband the fool just cursed and rejected the future king of Israel. Indeed, he had protected what was ours while he was in the hills, and now your husband rejected his request. Surely David will come and kill all of us!"

Abigail was no fool.

She knew something needed to be done.

She didn't go whining to Nabal, saying, "You fool, look what you have done! We are all going to die! You are an idiot!"

Nope.

She bravely moved with wisdom.

She gathered food—lots and lots and lots of it—to take to David.

So, now we have one contingency coming to seek revenge and one going out to seek peace.

The two meet.

Risking her own life, Abigail got off her donkey and fell at David's feet.

She said, "Master, I will take the blame. Don't look at Nabal. He really is a fool. You have every right to kill us, but I am asking you to receive the gifts I am bringing and to spare us."

She bravely took the path of love and peace, which is what allowed God to take the path of justice.

David looked at her and realized that she had been sent by God to stop him. This fight was not one that God had commissioned.

He blessed her and praised God that she had come to stop him from avenging himself with his own hand.

Abigail went home.

She told Nabal what she had done.

Ten days later Nabal dies.

Now she is "not married."

David, who is not a fool, knew a good thing when he saw it.

He asked Abigail to marry him.

She did.[2]

She was spit upon, ridiculed, laughed at and scorned.

She was called a witch and a baby killer.

Everywhere she turned, she faced repeated rejections.

She had lost the man she loved.

He, like most men of their generation, had not wanted a woman who thought for herself. He had been attracted and at the same time repulsed by her intelligence.

She was severely injured and became blind in one eye.

She was a woman courageously pioneering her way into an arena solely occupied by men.

If it had not been for a desperate plea from a dying friend and a supernatural divine revelation from God, she would surely have quit. But she didn't quit.

Instead, against all odds, Elizabeth Blackwell accomplished her dream. In 1847, she entered medical school and became America's first woman doctor.

She accomplished her dream by courageously focusing on *why* she was becoming a doctor.

At that time in history, poor women had virtually no health care.

Many died.

She was determined to change that.

So when she was ridiculed, when she felt fear from the threats of others, she tapped into the courage we have all been given and rose up as the warrior.

Today women of all generations have a lot to applaud Elizabeth Blackwell for.[3]

We will all face fear.

Overcoming it is our biggest battle.

Lots of people ask, "What if I mess up? What if I fail?"

And so the fear of failure keeps them from trying.

But I say, "Is there not a cause?"

Ashley Smith was afraid, but her sense of cause was greater.

Abigail was afraid as she fell before David, but the cause was more important.

Elizabeth Blackwell was afraid, but her fear paled in comparison to the cause.

Patrick Henry said that the "battle is not to the strong alone; it is to the vigilant, the active, the brave."[4]

The prophet Habakkuk said it best:

> The Lord God is my Strength,
> My personal bravery.
> And my invincible army;
> He makes my feet like hinds' feet and will make me to walk.
> Not stand still in terror, but to walk.
> And make spiritual progress upon my high places
> of trouble, suffering, or responsibility.[5]

I love that.

He is my strength and my bravery.

My invincible army.

Good to know.

Some have said that I was brave to share my breast cancer story so openly while still in the middle of the journey.

Maybe.

I just know one way to do life and that is *open*.

It is okay to be scared, as long as scared drives us to our knees.

David told his God, "When I cried out, You answered me and made me bold with strength in my soul."[6] Any courage I have is because I have tapped into the strength of my God.

Like David, I have discovered that when I call out to Him, He *makes* me bold.

In his book *The Warrior's Heart,* Harry R. Jackson describes the importance of knowing the cause. He says that Steven Spielberg's *Saving Private Ryan* portrayed the invasion of Normandy in a way that most of us hadn't seen before. The footage of the graphic violence of the landing on Omaha Beach was almost too real to watch. And I have heard that what actually happened was many times worse.

Hard to imagine.

In the movie, about 75 actors played parts in which they were "shot or wounded" landing on Omaha; and about 200 others were seen lying on the ground; and successfully getting through enemy defenses and off the beach took 26 minutes.

In 1944, in the real landing, it took 7 hours, more than 7,000 were killed and thousands more were wounded.

Was victory that day worth the enormous price?

Was the "why" worth it?

In light of history, the answer is a very painful yes.

No one is his right mind goes to war for fun, excitement or glory. There is great sacrifice, which must always be measured by the value of the mission.[7]

The "why."

We all have a "why" that will give us the courage to get through each and every battle.

In his book *First Things First,* author Stephen Covey wrote about Victor Frankl, an Austrian psychologist who survived the concentration camps of Nazi Germany. Frankl made a startling discovery about why some overcame the horrible conditions and why some did not.

> He looked at several factors—health, vitality, family structure, intelligence, survival skills. Finally, he concluded that

none of these factors was primarily responsible. The single most significant factor, he realized, <u>was a sense of future vision—the impelling conviction of those who were to survive that they had a mission to perform, some important work left to do</u>. Survivors of POW camps in Vietnam and elsewhere have reported similar experiences; a compelling, future-oriented vision is the primary force that kept many of them alive.[8]

So it is the compelling vision that moves us forward.

On a nonglobal scale . . .

Because of some hereditary issues, and an accident or two, I have spent countless hours in the dentist's office. A few years ago I had to undergo more dental work. Yuck. I put on my brave face and spent about seven hours in one sitting, with my mouth open and that little suction thingy (so technical, I know) making lots of noise. Oh, and let's not forget the sound of the high-pitched drill running for hours straight, the metal crown remover thumping in my head and needles being stuck in the roof of my mouth. Sounds like fun, doesn't it?

I bravely got through this process because of the "why."

The healthy and strong teeth I would have.

That was the "why."

It is not that bravehearts don't ever feel fear.

We do.

In living life on the earth we will encounter fear.

Fear of failure.

Fear of defeat.

Fear of the future.

Fear of the unknown.

Fear of the "what ifs."

Fear of people.

Fear of death.

Fear is debilitating.

Fear can stop us in our tracks.

Fear can keep us from fulfilling our purpose.

Fear is the ultimate weapon of the enemy as he seeks to prevent us from fulfilling our mission.

In all its forms, fear must be conquered.

Every hero of the Bible encountered fear.

And every one of them who praised their God destroyed the fear.

When they lifted their hands and voices to the great I AM.

David was a great warrior.

He was also known as the "sweet psalmist of Israel."

Great warriors know that their first response in any battle is to worship God.

Every modern-day hero—that would be you—encounters fear.

And we destroy it when we lift our voice to the King of kings.

When we praise our God, we are acknowledging His awesomeness, His majesty.

His kingdom and His cause.

We are acknowledging that He is God and we are not.

There's a thought.

If you and I just stay faithful to follow the path, the battle plan that our God has given, then we can rest in knowing that He is on the throne.

Keeping our focus on God destroys fear.

There is a phase every child must grow out of.

The "all about me" phase.

This is when we are concerned with our stuff, our hair, our clothes, our agenda, our way. When we focus on what we have and what we don't.

Those of you with children know exactly what I am talking about. This is the time when children aren't so concerned about the needs of the whole family, just their own needs. And as parents, one of our jobs is to help them mature out of this phase.

I wonder if God isn't waiting for some of us grown-up kids to make the same journey.

We must get to the place where we realize that everything we are has been designed to contribute to the mission God has sent us on.

It's not about us at all.

Again, it's about His kingdom and His cause.

> Maybe you are at a place in life where weariness and strain are more commonplace than rest and wonder.
>
> God knows you better than you know yourself.
>
> He knows just how small and frail you are.
>
> He knows you're just one person, and a tiny one at that.
>
> He knows all the things that you are not—and He made you that way for a purpose.
>
> That's why He has never asked you to be more than you are—little you with a great big God.

But God also is in touch with just how potent He is, desiring to do huge, God-sized things through you if you're ready to abandon the path of making more of self and embrace the miracle of being small, yet knowing His name.

It all starts when you look up.[9]

Are you afraid?

Turn your focus to Him and His cause.

I am not so sure the fear totally disappears—it just seems to because His cause is so much greater.

Remember the movie *The Lion King*?

Simba, the young cub, decided to do some exploring on his own.

He encountered those nasty hyenas that would have loved to eat him for lunch.

Simba stared them down and let out a little growl.

It was not a very intimidating one.

In fact, the hyenas just laughed.

Now Simba was afraid.

He cleared his throat and opened his mouth to roar again.

But instead of a squeaky little noise, a giant, powerful roar came out.

It actually wasn't his roar.

It was the roar of his very strong, very magnificent father standing behind him.

His little roar got swallowed up by a bigger one.

Our fears get swallowed up by a much bigger cause.

God, the awesome I AM, the one who created the universe with a word, chose to use mere mortals.

He chose to use men and women to complete His mission on Earth.

He still does.

He turns wounded souls into bravehearts.

Zeros into heroes.

He could have blasted Pharaoh off the planet, yet He chose an old man from the backside of nowhere to defeat Pharaoh, lead His people out of Egypt and into freedom.

He could have blown all the 'ites in the Promise Land off the map, and yet He chose Joshua, Saul, David and more to fight them.

He could destroy all the hunger and pain that exist on Earth today. And yet He chooses you and me to be His mouthpiece, His hands of mercy. He chooses to use us to extend His grace and bring His justice to a hurting world.

Earth time is short.

Eternity is long.

Really, you and I are just blips on the timeline of eternity.

And yet . . .

We are loved by the God who spoke the vast universe into being.

And He has a plan to use us to broadcast His name.

And it takes courage to lay down our ego.

Courage to do the right thing.

Courage to declare along with the prophet Isaiah that His name and His renown is the desire of our hearts.[10]

History is really just His story from beginning to end.

Sometimes it is hard to fathom.

You and I have been invited into the massive and mysterious story of the great I AM.[11]

We are His warriors on assignment.

It's not about us.

It's all about fulfilling His plan.

A wise man, in fact the wisest on the earth, said, "If you fall to pieces in a crisis, there wasn't much to you in the first place. Rescue the perishing; don't hesitate to step in and help. If you say, 'Hey, that's none of my business,' will that get you off the hook? Someone is watching you closely, you know—Someone not impressed with weak excuses."[12]

Okay.

So there is the "why."

We can't let fear cause us to draw back.

Why?

Because we are to rescue those who are perishing.

Someone you know does not need explanations—she needs someone to inspire her.

To be an example.

We can't even plead ignorance and say that we don't know she is perishing.

Doesn't look like our excuses will be believed.

I am not saying that we have to rescue every person around the planet. I do think we will be busy enough with the ones that come across our path.

Bravehearts.

That would be you and me.

We are here to make a difference in the world.

Not to point fingers about how corrupt and bad it is.

But to help.

To be a part of the solution.

God loved the world so much that He sent Jesus.

He sent His best.

Can we love enough to give our best?

Just a thought.

Humanity was created and placed in the middle of creation. The first man and woman were commanded to lovingly care for it, manage it and to creatively order it.

From day one, which is actually day six, they were in intimate relationship with their environment. They were environmentalists.[13]

Is that thought shocking to you?

You and I are to take care of our part of the planet.

Which is why I think litter and pollution are spiritual issues.

Instead of complaining about how bad it all is, why don't we begin to do something?

Plant trees.

Recycle.

Reduce our energy use.

Got any other ideas?

Another thought.

I sometimes wonder if it doesn't actually hinder the gospel going forth when Christians picket and boycott and complain about how bad the world is.

I am not sure this behavior helps.

It might just make it worse.

I don't think it is the kind of voice Jesus wants His followers to have in the world.

Why blame the dark for being dark?

It is far more helpful to ask why the light isn't as bright as it could be.[14]

> In many ways, the twenty-first century Church is under assault by the culture. And perhaps as a result of the attack against our beliefs and principles, our concept of righteousness is centered on personal holiness and our personal standing before God. In other words, in many cases we have begun to evaluate righteousness in terms of the negatives we should avoid instead of the power we were meant to create in the earth. David said that "righteousness and justice are the foundation" of God's throne. So I would think this means that God's power will be truly demonstrated when personal righteousness is embraced and an atmosphere of social justice is created.
>
> America's First Great Awakening occurred when John and Charles Wesley preached salvation along with abolition of slavery. Sometimes this commitment to social justice is what is missing among today's Christ followers.[15]

This needs to change.

You and I need to become people who promote, release and create justice.

David challenges us to "defend the cause of the weak and fatherless; maintain the rights of the poor and oppressed."[16]

As Rob Bell likes to remind us, "The church doesn't exist for itself; it exists to serve the world. It is not ultimately about the church; it's about all the people God wants to bless through the church. When the church loses sight of this, it loses its heart."[17]

God is letting us know that we have a responsibility to carry out justice as a way of glorifying Him. Heaven's courts always pay attention to injustice, and to those who are committed to countering the injustice with justice.[18]

Sometimes it is fear that can cause us to draw back from our mission to execute justice.

And sometimes it is indifference.

Indifference to what is going on around us.

Indifference to the hurting.

Indifference to the needs of people.

Warriors are not indifferent to what is going on around them.

We might say, "Oh, I am going to rest . . . take a break."

That is fine.

We just have to be honest with ourselves and admit when taking a break turns into sitting out the battle.

Jesus was not very impressed with those believers who were lukewarm.

And when we enter into the lukewarm danger zone, we find that we don't care much about anything.

Not hurting people.

Not lost people.

And not the mission for which we have been created.

Be careful.

Being content is good. Content with today. Content with what we have.

But I don't think being satisfied is ever good. Being satisfied can lead to slowing down, which can lead to stopping, which can lead to lukewarmness.

Not good.

I think the opposite of indifference, of being lukewarm, is passion.

Being indifferent, being passive, can get us in trouble.

King David found this out.

One spring when all kings were supposed to be in battle, David decided to stay home.

And then he just lazed around in bed all day.

When he arose in the evening, he saw a beautiful woman taking a bath.

She was Bathsheba.

And most of us know the end of that story.

Could it be that his passivity, his staying home when he should have been at war, opened the door to temptation—which then led to adultery and murder?

We had seen David be courageous and passionate as he ran toward Goliath and as he led his troops.

And yet.

Like all of us, when he backed off and let indifference to the cause of His God take over, trouble came.

We really are warriors.

We can't ever forget that.

And warriors are passionate.

Passion is contagious.

Passion motivates.

When William Wallace was rallying his troops to fight the British, not only did he have blue war paint on, he was also passionate. In the movie *Braveheart,* he was portrayed as being eloquent as well, but I would imagine that in real life William Wallace's passion surpassed his eloquence.

Battle cries are not uttered as an afterthought.

They are shouted with passion.

The battle cry itself helps stir up the passion—which builds the necessary courage.

Before every major battle, commanders motivate their troops with passionate speech. They remind them of the cause and the reason they are in this fight. No warrior casually heads into battle.

It is passion that stirs up the "fight" in all of us.

I have seen many people lose battles simply because the fight has gone out of them.

I have seen people fighting illness who simply yielded.

I am not judging.

I know how tiring it can be to fight disease.

But cancer is not a casual disease.

It is an aggressive monster.

And it must be fought with passion and aggression.

Left alone, most things will become just average.

Including marriage.

If we want a great marriage, we are going to have to fight for it.

And that will require passion.

I am not just talking about sex.

Although that is certainly important! (And fun.)

I am talking about passionately learning, forgiving, trying.

As soon as we back off, our marriage becomes just average—nothing special. And then the downward spiral begins.

Pastoring a church requires passion.

Over the course of 24 years, we have had some challenges in the church. And every time it is a passionate vision that gets us through. Plans and budgets are certainly important, and yet, it is communicating the vision with passion that brings victory.

Winning basketball games requires passion too.

I watched my daughter and her team play the other day.

Her team was playing a team they had soundly beaten twice before.

Unfortunately, they approached this new game as if victory were guaranteed.

They were careless.

They made lazy passes.

They let the other team drive by them to score one time too many.

They lost.

Reaching a dream requires passion.

Sitting on the couch for hours watching television instead of actively pursuing our dream is not going to bring the results we want.

Sitting on the bleachers, just watching, while others pursue their dreams will only bring us frustration.

Just hoping our dreams come to pass is not going to do it.

We will need a plan.

And we will need to stir up the passion within us to put that plan into action.

Fulfilling our purpose will require passion.

The passion to overcome obstacles.

The passion to persevere.

It will take passion to reach the finish line and hear, "Well done."

Bringing justice will require passion.

The passion to not only see the need but to also do something about it.

The passion to rally our fellow warriors into making a difference.

It will take passion to keep His cause first and foremost.

It will take passion to make His name famous.

In a scene from *Return of the King*, Aragorn tries to inspire his very out-numbered men to fight against what seems like sure defeat. Hell's swarming legions have gathered before them and the courage of Aragorn's fighters is weakening. Riding along the front lines of his discouraged army, he shouts:

> I see in your eyes the same fear that would take the heart of me. A day may come when the courage of men fails, when we forsake our friends and break all bonds of fellow-ship. But it is not this day . . . this day we fight![19]

Some Last Thoughts

Warrior.

You.

Can you see yourself that way?

I hope so.

I am hoping that somehow my words have encouraged you to live your life as the warrior you are.

You are His beauty.

Beautiful.

Just the way you are.

I do not know what situations of life you find yourself in, but can you rise?

Can you get up?

Even when it is hard.

Others around you may be giving up.

But you don't have to.

Rise, warrior, rise.

When the battle is raging, it is hard sometimes to just stand.

To stay at our posts.

You can do it.

Don't abandon your assignments.

No matter how hard it gets.

People are watching as we stay at our post.

Maybe we all have a little bit of Attention Deficit Disorder.

Because we can all lose focus.

We can all lose sight of where we were headed.

But warriors need to remember what they are here for.

Focus on what we are going to—not just what we are going through.

Eyeballs!

(Did that help?)

Okay, old woman.

There is a baton exchange coming.

Are you ready?

Can you share a piece of your life with a young woman?

And don't forget to extend your hand to that older woman.

She has a baton to hand to you.

The really great thing about living life as a warrior is that we really are never alone.

There are women whose strengths make our platoon better.

How are you doing with the whole "together" thing?

Is your heart open to His house and His people?

You will be stronger when your strength is partnered up with that of others.

Together.

Are you dressed?

Warriors are very familiar with their armor.

We don't just hang it in the closet.

We put it on.

The sword of the warrior does not rest on the mantle.

It is used every day.

How's that coming for you?

Yielding to authority certainly is not everyone's favorite subject.

But warriors understand that we must yield.

That to have authority, they must be under it.

Are you using the authority you have been given?

Please do.

It will make our platoon stronger.

Warriors are in constant training.

Constant.

Managing our bodies.

Managing our health.

Alert to what is going on around us.

Growing in our ability to handle situations.

Because we are in this for the long haul.

Warriors make the journey.

From victim to overcomer.

We know there are so many people we have been called to help.

So we must overcome.

The "why."

Probably the most important thought:

We are not warriors for ourselves alone, but so that we can make a difference in our world.

God plucked us out of eternity and put us at this time in history.

It is no accident.

We are here now.

And we have a mission.

It is to be a liberator.

Jesus came to release captives.

And that is our job too.

There are plenty of people in your world and mine who are bound.

Who are wearing handcuffs.

Maybe not the steel kind.

But maybe they are bound by hunger.

Maybe they are bound with guilt.

Maybe they are bound by illiteracy.

They might be bound by fear.

Maybe it is poverty.

And the awesome thing is . . . you and I have been entrusted with the key to release them.

The key.

The key could be food . . . and then teaching how to grow it.

Or the truth of forgiveness.

Or taking the time to teach someone to read.

Or it might simply be money.

Let's complete our mission as liberators, so that together we will hear, "Well done."

warrior chicks study guide

Chapter 1

1. What battle are you fighting?

2. How does it feel to be in this battle?

3. "A soldier signs up to join the fight, a warrior stays until it is finished." How can you stay committed to your battle?

4. List the lies you hear in your head ("I don't deserve to be loved," "I am not pretty," "My marriage won't make it"). Next to every lie, write God's truth ("I was bought with a price," "I am fearfully and wonderfully made," "My husband rejoices with the bride of his youth").

5. Is there someone in your life that you compare yourself to? Why?

6. How can you be inspired by her instead of comparing yourself to her?

7. Remember the cracked pot story? How can your past struggles and issues create a garden for others to enjoy?

8. Find the closest mirror. Look at your cute face. Now, pick up your megaphone and shout, "I am fearfully and wonderfully made! *And how well I know it!*"

9. If your neighbor stopped by to make sure you're okay, invite her in to do the same! ☺

Chapter 2

1. Read Psalm 139. Focus on verses 11 and 12. How can the darkness of your situation appear as light?

2. Consider your trial(s). How can you "rise while it is yet night"?

3. Who is a woman from the past or present whose life challenges you to rise? Imagine that she is cheering you on.

4. What lesson from her own life would she share with you?

5. Who is watching you fight your battles? Your daughter? Your coworker? Your friend? List everyone who is following your lead.

6. How do you feel knowing they are watching?

7. Pick one of the people you just listed (see question 5). Focus on that person in prayer for a moment. Now, call and encourage her in her situation.

Chapter 3

1. To what posts have you been assigned?

2. When have you been tempted to abandon one of them? (Remember my earthquake story!)

3. How has the decision not to abandon it affected your life?

4. Is there a post you are tempted to leave right now?

5. How can you rekindle the enthusiasm, the passion, with which you first began serving at this post?

6. Is there an older woman in your life who stayed at her post? Give her a call. Thank her for staying and then ask her for wisdom.

7. Meditate on 2 Corinthians 6:3-10 this week. Let these life-giving words encourage you to keep going.

Chapter 4

1. Think of a time in your life when you lost your focus. Was it in your marriage? Your Christian walk?

2. What were the steps you took to regain your focus?

3. Is there a present area in which your focus is beginning to drift? How can you apply those same steps in your life now (include yelling, "Eyeballs!")?

4. "A person focused in the present exercises today . . ." What have you said "maybe one day . . ." about?

5. What can you do *today*?

6. "Good is the enemy of the best." List your responsibilities. Can you tell which ones are "good" and which ones are "best"?

7. What temptations are currently distracting you?

8. In spite of what you are going *through*, how can you focus on what you are going *to*?

Chapter 5

1. Who is the older woman in your world? How have you opened up your life to her?

2. Who is the younger woman in your world? How have you opened up your life to her?

3. What challenge have you overcome in your life that you could use to encourage someone younger?

4. How do you feel about being called an "old woman?" (smile)

Chapter 6

1. How do you feel about doing life "together"?

2. Who are your battle partners?

3. What are some of the gifts God has given you?

4. How can you work together with others to use your gifts in the house of God?

5. Remember my jeans story? Think of a time when God gave you what you needed, right at the moment you needed it.

6. Describe the lane you are running in.

7. Think of a friend running next to you. Now, think of your other friend who is really weird (the one with the exact opposite personality). How can you encourage her to stay in her lane?

8. Okay, now go do it!

9. Is there someone you need to forgive? I know it's hard, but why don't you forgive that person in such a way that you inspire her to say, "When I saw your face, it was as the face of God smiling on me."

Chapter 7

1. Do you tend to have a romantic or realistic view of life?

2. How has that hurt you or helped you in the past?

3. Read Esther 4. Are you having a cruise-ship moment during a battleship moment? How can you be like Esther and step up for a time such as this?

4. Wearing the helmet of salvation reminds us who we are. What are some Scriptures that remind you who you are?

5. The breastplate of righteousness protects our hearts and reminds us we are right with God (without having to earn it!). What steps can you take to guard your heart?

6. Is your belt of truth on? Come on! It looks cute with those jeans!

7. What resources could help you hear, read and understand the Word of God more clearly?

8. Read Psalm 119:165. Pray for the shoes of peace to cover your cute pedicure. Now, take it one step further and pray peace into the lives of those closest to you.

9. Remember a time when the shield of faith was all you had. Thank God for His faithfulness.

Chapter 8

1. Picture Jesus in the Garden of Gethsemane. What does His submission to the Father mean for you? How does it make you feel to know He loves you so much that He was willing to yield His life for you?

2. Can you lay down your agenda, your time, your love and yield for the sake of the well-being of others?

3. We have been given authority to make decisions. Name a time you made a decision that was not the best for your life. How did that affect your life?

4. Name a time you made a great decision. How did that choice enrich your life and the lives of those around you?

5. What do you really need in your life? Forgiveness, affection at home, friendship? How can you begin to sow the seed that will yield a rich harvest of what you need?

6. "We cannot dwell on what will not produce life." What thoughts do you need to take captive?

7. Whose authority have you been placed under (that of your husband, boss, church director, pastor)? Is it hard for you to yield?

8. Read Hebrews 11. Can you have faith just for today?

9. If yielding to authority is a great display of faith, what do you have on display?

Chapter 9

1. In what area are you currently training?

2. What kind of focus has that required?

3. Since mistakes are inevitable, how can you offer yourself grace while training?

4. What have you done right as a parent (and yes, there is at least one thing!)?

5. Can you add to your daily routine one thing that will lead you toward optimum health? (Like drinking two more glasses of water or maybe a shot of wheatgrass?)

6. Be aware of the world around you. Is there anything you should pay more attention to?

7. What is in your hand that seems little? How can you be faithful so that God can increase your capacity?

Chapter 10

1. What have you been a victim of?

2. What did you do to survive?

3. Will you make the decision to overcome?

4. What will that take?

5. One way to begin the journey as an overcomer is to help others who have been through a similar ordeal survive. Name someone in your life whom you can help.

6. Think of a situation right now in which you are a victim or a survivor. How can you be an overcomer?

7. Call your friend and tell her your story.

Chapter 11

1. How does Ashley Smith's story make you feel?

2. Are you afraid?

3. How does that fear hold you back?

4. Can you let the cause be larger than the fear?

5. What is your purpose?

6. What is your "why"?

7. Picture a girl or young woman who is watching you live your life. She is your "why." Call her and encourage her on her journey.

8. What are some ways you can stir up the passion within you?

9. What is one way you can take care of your part of the planet?

10. Is there an area of life in which you feel a little indifferent? How is that affecting you?

Endnotes

Chapter 1: *Bellisima!*
1. Michelle Graham, *Wanting to Be Her*, (Downers Grove, IL: Intervarsity Press, 2005), p.16.
2. Psalm 139:14, *CEV*.
3. "The Cracked Pot," a tale from India. Retold by Mark Dessein at www.healingstory.org. http://www.healingstory.org/treasure/cracked_pot/cracked_pot.html (accessed April 2007).
4. See Ephesians 2:10.
5. Sun Tzu, *The Art of War*, book 3, c. 500 B.C., tr. Giles, 1910, as quoted in *Greenhill Dictionary* (London: Greenhill Books, new ed. 2006), p. 502.

Chapter 2: Rise and Shine!
1. See John 16:33, *AMP*.
2. Second Corinthians 2:14.
3. See Isaiah 60:1.
4. Margot Morrell and Stephanie Capparell, *Shackleton's Way* (London: Nicholas Brealy Publishing, 2001).
5. Dan and Michelle Lutz, "I Rise," Chris James, producer, © Landutz Music, Northridge, CA. Used by permission.
6. See Judges 5:7.
7. Esther 4:14, *NIV*.
8. See Hebrews 12:1.
9. See Proverbs 24:10, *AMP*.
10. James 1:2-4.
11. First Samuel 30:4-6.
12. See 1 Samuel 30:7-8.
13. See Acts 16:25.
14. See 2 Timothy 2:3.
15. Winston Churchill, "We Shall Fight on the Beaches," speech to the House of Commons, June 4, 1940.

Chapter 3: Stay at Your Post!
1. Second Chronicles 20:21.
2. Second Timothy 4:7, *NIV*.
3. John Stephen Akhwari, as quoted in Bud Greenspan, *100 Greatest Moments in Olympic History* (Toronto, Canada: Stoddart Publishing, 1995).
4. See Hebrews 12:2.

Chapter 4: Focus!
1. Scott Jette, Corps Wisdom (Enumclaw, WA: WinePress Publishing, 2007), p. 15.
2. Ibid., p. 16.
3. Ibid., p. 17.
4. "Louis Pasteur," History Learning Site. http://www.historylearningsite.co.uk/louis_pasteur.htm (accessed April 2007).
5. See Mark 8:16-21.

Chapter 5: The Baton Exchange
1. "Baton Blunder Costs USA," BBC Online, August 27, 2004. http://news.bbc.co.uk/sport1/hi/olympics_2004/athletics/3603300.stm (accessed April 2007).
2. Susan B. Anthony in a speech given in 1864, quoted in Lynn Scherr, *Failure Is Impossible: Susan B. Anthony in Her Own Words* (New York: Random House, 1995).

Chapter 6: Never Alone
1. First Corinthians 12:5.
2. General George S. Patton, quoted in U.S. Senator Robert Torricelli, ed., *Quotations for Public Speakers* (New Brunswick, NJ: Rutgers University Press, 2001), p. 259.
3. See Psalm 92:13.

4. First Timothy 3:15, *NIV.*
5. See 1 Corinthians 3:6; 4:8.
6. First Corinthians 12:14-24.
7. Genesis 33:10.

Chapter 7: Get Dressed!
1. Esther 4:13-14.
2. Holly Wagner, *Daily Steps for GodChicks* (Ventura, CA: Regal Publishers, 2005), p. 92.
3. Ibid.
4. See Proverbs 4:23.
5. Wagner, *Daily Steps for GodChicks*, p. 87.
6. Ibid., p. 86.
7. Ephesians 6:15, *NIV.*
8. Wagner, *Daily Steps for GodChicks,* p. 87.
9. Ibid., p. 88.
10. See Ecclesiastes 9:11, *NIV.*
11. See Proverbs 24:16, *NIV.*
12. See Habakkuk 2:4, *KJV.*
13. Matthew 4:10, *NIV.*
14. First Samuel 17:45-47.
15. See Proverbs 6:2-3.
16. Wagner, *Daily Steps for GodChicks,* p. 95.
17. See Exodus 15:26, *NIV.*
18. See Psalm 91:16, *NIV.*
19. Psalm 118:6, *NIV.*
20. See Psalm 91:5,7.
21. See Isaiah 54:17, *CEV.*
22. See Deuteronomy 28:13, *NIV.*
23. See Malachi 3:10, *NKJV.*
24. See Philippians 4:19, *NKJV.*
25. See John 10:10, *NIV.*
26. Hebrews 13:4, *NKJV.*
27. See Proverbs 5:18, *NKJV.*
28. See 2 Corinthians 12:9-10, *NLT.*
29. See Ephesians 6:10.

Chapter 8: Who's the Boss?
1. See Deuteronomy 30:19.
2. See Matthew 9:6.
3. See 2 Corinthians 9:6.
4. See 2 Corinthians 10:5, *NIV.*
5. See Proverbs 23:7, *NKJV.*
6. See Hebrews 13:17, *NIV.*
7. Holly Wagner, *Dumb Things She Does* (Nashville, TN: Thomas Nelson Publishers, 2002), pp. 37-39.
8. See Proverbs 29:18, *AMP.*
9. Psalm 5:8.
10. See Ephesians 1:10.
11. See Matthew 6:34, *NIV.*
12. Harry R. Jackson Jr, *The Warrior's Heart* (Grand Rapids, Michigan: Chosen Books, 2004), p. 25.
13. Ibid., p. 197.
14. Byron Pitts, quoted in Jackson, *The Warrior's Heart*, p. 195.
15. Jackson, *The Warrior's Heart,* p. 196.
16. Matthew 8:8-10,13, *NIV.*

Chapter 9: Ready or Not . . .
1. Gene Edwards, *Tale of Three Kings* (Carol Stream, IL: Tyndale House Publishers, 1992), pp. 4-5.

2. *Dictionary.com Unabridged (v 1.1)*, s.v. "train," Dictionary.com. http://dictionary.refer ence.com/browse/train (accessed April 2007).
3. Michael Jordan, quoted at http://www.brainyquote.com/quotes/quotes/m/ michaeljor127660.html (accessed April 2007).
4. Jeremiah 12:5.
5. See Proverbs 22:6, *NIV.*
6. *Dictionary.com Unabridged (v 1.1)*, s.v. "train," Dictionary.com. http://dictionary.ref erence.com/browse/train (accessed April 2007).
7. Dr. Myron Wentz, *Invisible Miracles* (Scottsdale, AZ: Medicis, Inc, 2002), p. 8.
8. *The Surgeon General's Report on Nutrition and Health,* U.S. Department of Health and Human Services (Public Health Service), 1988.
9. Proverbs 31:17, *AMP.*
10. First Corinthians 9:27, *AMP.*
11. See Judges 7 for the rest of this story!
12. *Dictionary.com Unabridged (v 1.1)*, s.v. "vigilant," Dictionary.com. http://dictionary. reference.com/browse/vigilant (accessed April 2007).
13. See 1 Peter 5:8, *AMP.*
14. Holly Wagner, *GodChicks* (Nashville, TN: Thomas Nelson, 2003), p. 190.
15. See Matthew 25:14-29.
16. See Hebrews 12:1.

Chapter 10: More Than
1. The American Heritage® Dictionary of the English Language, fourth edition, s.v. "victim." Houghton Mifflin Company, 2004. http://dictionary.reference.com/browse/ victim (accessed April 2007).
2. Immaculee Ilibagiza, *Left to Tell* (Carlsbad, California: Hay House, Inc, 2006).
3. Romans 8:37, *AMP.*
4. See Romans 8:35, *AMP.*
5. See Philippians 3:13, *NKJV.*
6. See 2 Corinthians 1:4.

Chapter 11: Braveheart
1. Information from Ashley Smith Bio at Premiere Speakers Bureau, http://premiere-speakers.com/ashley_smith/bio (accessed April 2007), and "Ex-hostage: 'I wanted to gain his trust,'" www.cnn.com/2005/LAW/03/14/smith.transcript/ (accessed April 2007).
2. Check out 1 Samuel 25 for all the details!
3. Holly Wagner, *GodChicks* (Nashville, TN: Thomas Nelson Publishers, 2003), pp. 36-37.
4. Patrick Henry, "Liberty or Death," in a speech delivered before the Virginia House of Burgesses on March 23, 1775. http://www.historyplace.com/unitedstates/revo lution/henry.htm (accessed April 2007).
5. See Habakkuk 3:19, *AMP.*
6. Psalm 138:3, *NKJV.*
7. Harry R. Jackson Jr., *The Warrior's Heart* (Grand Rapids, MI: Chosen Books, 2004), p. 68.
8. Stephen Covey, *First Things First* (New York: Free Press, 1996).
9. Louie Giglio, *I Am Not But I Know I AM* (Sisters, OR: Multnomah Publishers, 2005), p. 23.
10. See Isaiah 26:8.
11. See Isaiah 41.
12. Proverbs 24:10-12.
13. Rob Bell, *Velvet Elvis* (Grand Rapids, MI: Zondervan, 2005), p. 158.
14. Ibid., p. 166.
15. Jackson, *The Way of the Warrior*, p. 79.
16. Psalm 82:3, *NIV.*
17. Bell, *Velvet Elvis*, p. 165
18. Jackson, *The Way of the Warrior*, p. 80.
19. Francis Frangipane, *This Day We Fight!* (Grand Rapids, MI: Chosen, 2006), p. 32.

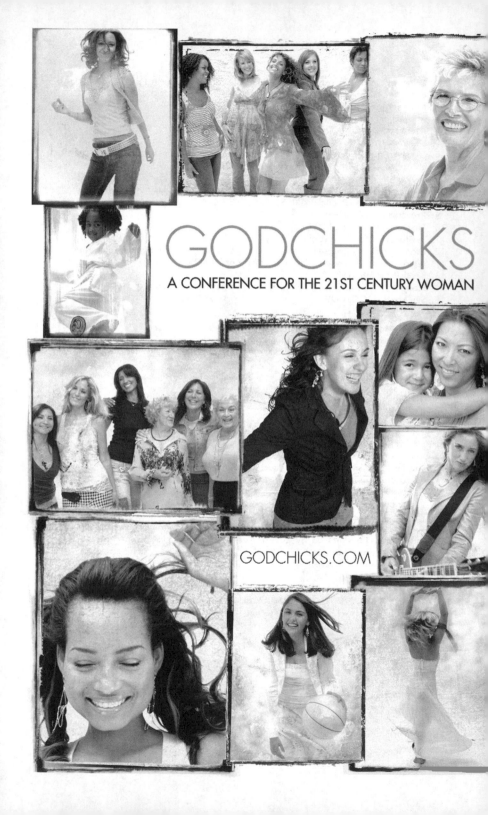

GODCHICKS

A CONFERENCE FOR THE 21ST CENTURY WOMAN

GODCHICKS.COM